D1460398

NOAH WEBSTER
1758 - 1843

PICTORIAL WEBSTER'S

Pocket Dictionary

G. & C. MERRIAM DICTIONARY ENGRAVINGS
OF THE NINETEENTH CENTURY PRINTED
ALPHABETICALLY AS A SOURCE FOR
CREATIVITY IN THE HUMAN BRAIN

JOHN M. CARRERA

AUTHOR, COMPOSER, PRINTER

CHRONICLE BOOKS
SAN FRANCISCO

Text copyright © 2012 by John M. Carrera

QUERCUS PRESS

Original edition of *Pictorial Webster's* © 2007 by John M. Carrera
All rights reserved. No part of this book may be reproduced in any form without written permission from the publisher.

Library of Congress Cataloging-in-Publication Data available.

ISBN: 978-1-4521-0164-4
Manufactured in China.

Cover Design and Typesetting by Eloise Leigh

10 9 8 7 6 5 4 3 2 1

Chronicle Books LLC
680 Second Street
San Francisco, CA 94107

INTRODUCTION

In the summer of 1995, while poking around my grandmother's stone farmhouse, I found a tattered 1898 *Webster's International Dictionary* under my grandfather's favorite reading chair. The disintegrating sheepskin covers were detached and a number of browned and brittle sections were falling out from the back of the book. The loose pages revealed an eighty-page section devoted entirely to the illustrations of the dictionary: a stunning array of odd and wonderful animals and machines printed by categories. The fantastic variety of subjects was matched only by the detail and variety of engraving techniques.

Shortly before discovering that fateful *Webster's*, I had completed a collaborative artist's book for an exhibit at the Dibner Library at the Smithsonian Institution that grappled with questions of the origin of ideas. I realized a book filled with disparate images, such as those from the *Webster's*, could be an artistic experiment to test my hypothesis on the origin of creativity: that new ideas arise from the recombinations of old ideas. It would also be an important and beautiful visual reference. That fall I embarked on a ten-year odyssey that culminated in a book called *Pictorial Webster's*; printed by hand on a letterpress from the original engravings and bound by hand and sold to institutions and collectors for $3,500. I then worked with Chronicle Books to make *Pictorial Webster's: A Visual Dictionary of Curiosities* which was a perfected version of the same book with additional essays written about the engravers and the history of dictionary illustration in America. This was printed and bound as a pleasing volume with a cover price of $35.00. But the editors at Chronicle Books felt that the public might still want something more affordable and accessible. When I was approached about making a "pocket sized," version of *Pictorial Webster's* I bristled. "The book is what it is. I've spent over a decade of my life on this project already," I thought.

Then I saw the dummy of the book the great designers at Chronicle had in mind and it was like the experience I had when I first saw the engravings in their dusty cases in the dark, cool basement of the Sterling Library at Yale University. I was immediately smitten with the size and heft of the little book. I carried it around with me in my back pocket and pulled it out whenever I could to admire it. I started laying images within the pages and realized the smaller-sized book would challenge me to create an even more powerful distillation of the book. And I started thinking: "Who says I got it right the first time, anyway? And wouldn't it be fun to try another way of organizing the images?" I remembered the very first dummy I made for the book was closer to this same size. "Yes, small is beautiful. Good design is elemental."

Although fewer in number than in *Pictorial Webster's*, the engravings in this work are reproduced from the nineteenth-century engravings used in Webster's Dictionaries printed by the G. & C. Merriam Co. (George and Charles Merriam bought the rights to the official "Webster's" in 1847, four years after Noah Webster died.) These engravings were borrowed from the 10,000 plus engravings and their exact metal duplicates called electrotypes held by the Arts of the Book Collection at Yale University. Wood engravings are created through a reduction process on the end-grain of boxwood using sharp little tools called burins. Boxwood is soft, but has incredibly dense grain, which allows for great detail. To print the engravings, ink is rolled onto the carved block then that block is pressed into the paper. The images in the book span two distinctive eras in American wood engraving. Black Line engravings, also called American Style, are made by making or transferring a line drawing directly onto the face of the boxwood. Then, using variously shaped burins, the engraver carves away all the wood except for the lines of the drawing. Well-known engraver, John Andrew, was hired to make the engravings for the 1859 and 1864 *Webster's*. What is forgotten today is that each line in Black Line engravings was imbued with meaning. As Hiram Merrill, an apprentice in John Andrew's shop, explained:

> *[W]ood engraving was held within limits established by tradition: a certain kind of line for skies, another for flesh, hair, foliage, drapery, water, rocks, foreground, background, etc., all with meaning and beauty in themselves. Once a line was cut it must not be modified in any way, and such a thing as cutting across the lines was regarded with horror.*

By the time the *International Dictionary* was printed in 1890, the New School of engraving was ubiquitous in America. Notable for its use of photographic methods to transfer images, the New School engravings have a more scientific and clinical feel to them. The old horror of cutting across the line is gone, as the emphasis of the New School was not line but tone.

After *Webster's New International Dictionary* was published in 1909, the engraving process was abandoned. Images that were new to the 1934 *Webster's New International Dictionary*, Second Edition and the 1961 *Webster's Third New International Dictionary* were printed from mounted copper plates made from line drawings. These later cuts make an interesting contrast to the wood engravings, not only for their content but also for their style and execution. The key following this introduction explains the letters that accompany each image indicating in which dictionary each engraving originally appeared.

The Pocket *Pictorial Webster's* can be enjoyed as a Portable Wonder Cabinet of Nineteenth-Century America. It is filled with both the factual and the fantastic. Like a surrealists collection of fabulous objects, collected to prompt the unconscious flow of ideas, this book may be used to unlock your own innermost thoughts or help spark your imagination. Humans instinctively look for connections between proximal objects. When you study a page, your brain immediately starts finding commonalities to find some way to link the various objects. The thread that connects them is often something new that you have never before considered. The farther removed two things are, the wilder the thread that connects them, but often the more powerful the idea. Because, truly, everything in the universe is connected somehow: it's just a question of figuring out the connection.

When the reader opens a page of this book to an image for which he or she has a particular association, that engraving may start as the focus of the page. Then, by associating unknown images into the context of the known one, that page will begin to develop a story. The titles are supplied to give names and subtext to the images. The numbers create a numerical tag, a tether to a deeper order of the universe. The more time you spend immersed in the pages, the more meaningful the book will become.

While making this book, I was awed, thinking of the great change that occurred during the Nineteenth and Twentieth centuries when humans evolved from creatures moving within the natural element of the world, to seeming conquerors. Holding images of endangered species and now outdated technology that took hour upon hour to engrave on my almost obsolete computer, I wonder if our march of materialism is leading us to greater happiness or harm. Perhaps our time is similar to the turn of the Twentieth century, which produced the fauvists and cubists, and I return to a dream that the world might be saved by creativity. Perhaps spending time in these pages of the time when it all seemed to change will help you come to your own solution. However you choose to read it, I hope you find much pleasure and inspiration exploring and studying the images, the pages, and the universe they create.

J. M. C.

URBANA, MARYLAND, 2011

KEY TO THE NUMBERS AND LETTERS ACCOMPANYING THE ENGRAVINGS

The notation following the "index number" below each image tells more about each engraving (for more about the "index numbers" see page 206):

W – denotes images printed directly from wood engraving blocks.

M – denotes images printed from metal electrotypes.

D – denotes images digitally captured and added for this trade edition.

The following letters and numbers are used to indicate the first edition of the dictionary in which the image appears:

I – denotes engravings the *Imperial Dictionary* of 1851.

9 – denotes the 1859 *American Dictionary of the English Language* .

4 – denotes the 1864 edition.

N – denotes the 1890 *International Dictionary.*

L – denotes an edition printed after 1900.

(Note that because this book was designed digitally, the author took liberty to flip or resize some of the images.)

A

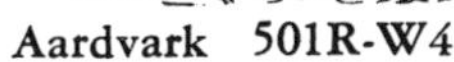

Aardvark 501R-W4

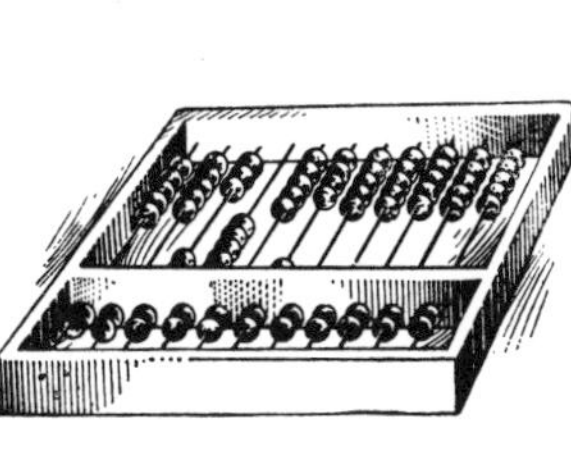

Abacus 617R-ML

Accipiter 415-W

A

Addax 312R-MN

Adze 203R-W4

Aeolipyle 302R-MN

Affrontee
319R-WI

Agouty 305R-W4

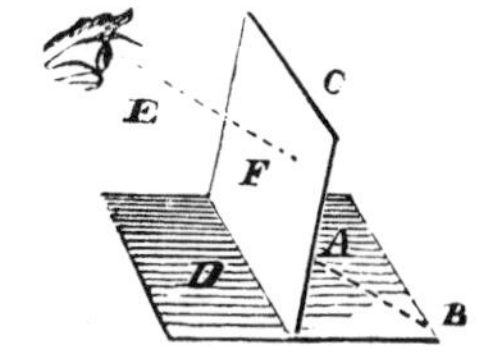

Accidental
Point 404R-W4

Aim
317R-MN

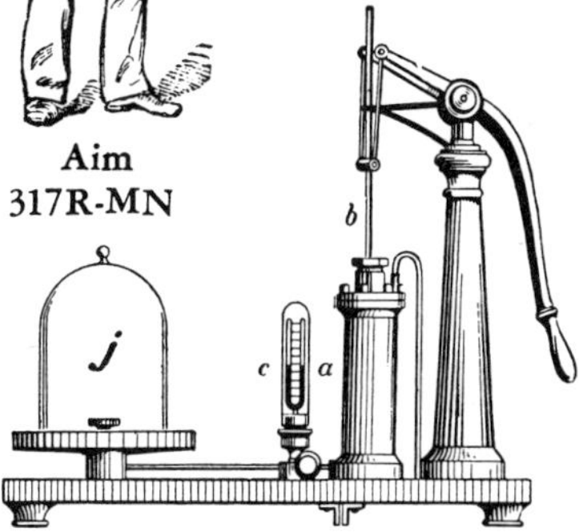

b
c
a
j

Air Pump 515R-MN

Akkad 913-ML

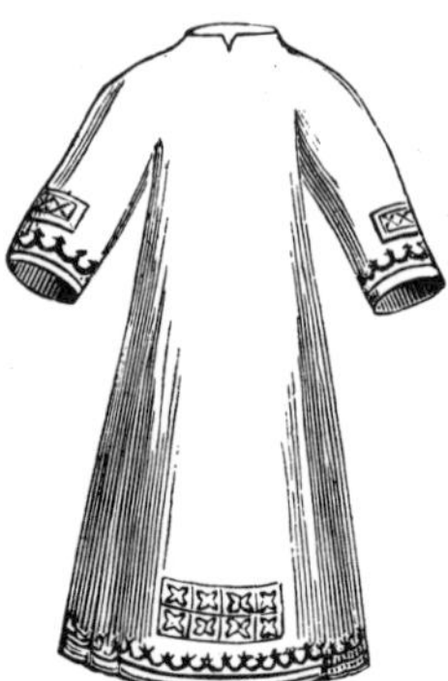

Alb 502R-W4

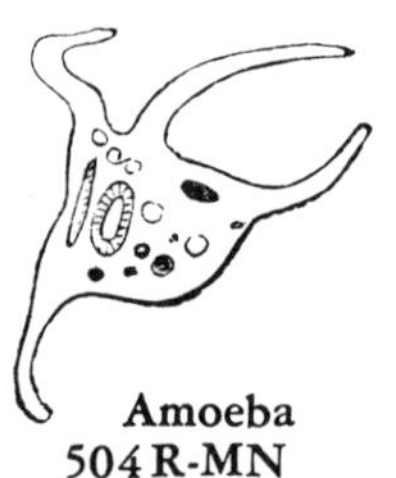

Amoeba
504R-MN

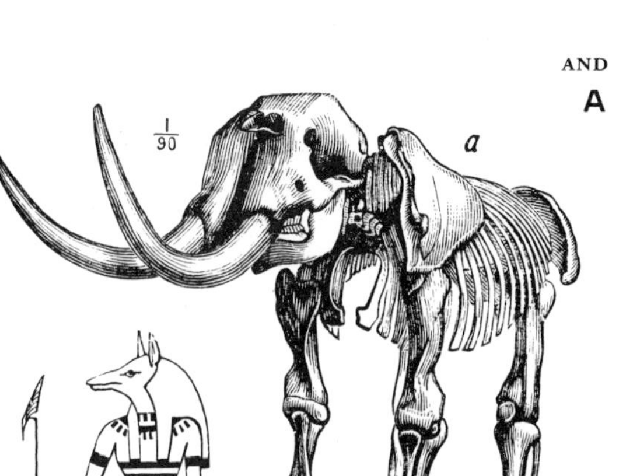

American Mastodon
207R-MN

Anubis 301R-W4

Anchor 413R-W4

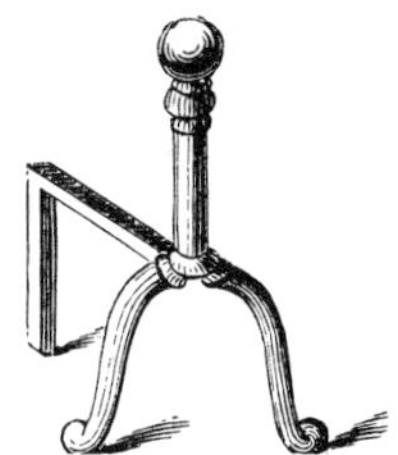

Andiron 313-W4

A

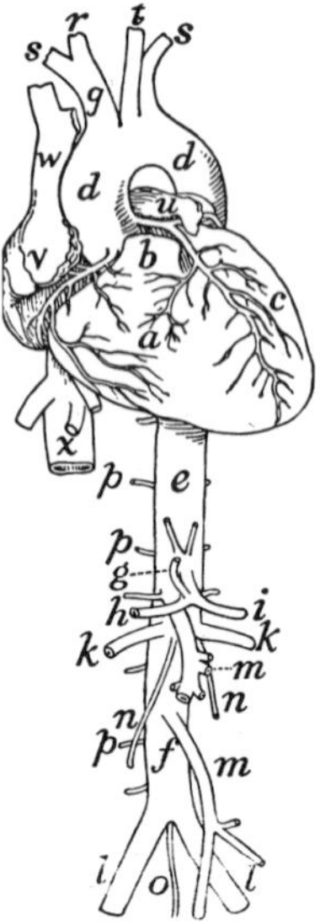

Aorta 601-MN

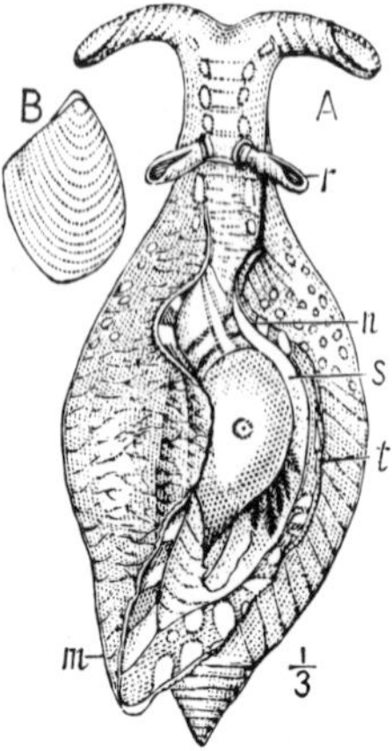

Aplysia 402R-MN

Aqueduct 603R-W4

Armillary Sphere 201-DI

Arrow 216R-W4

Armor
212R-M4

Ark of the Covenant 717-D4

ART

A

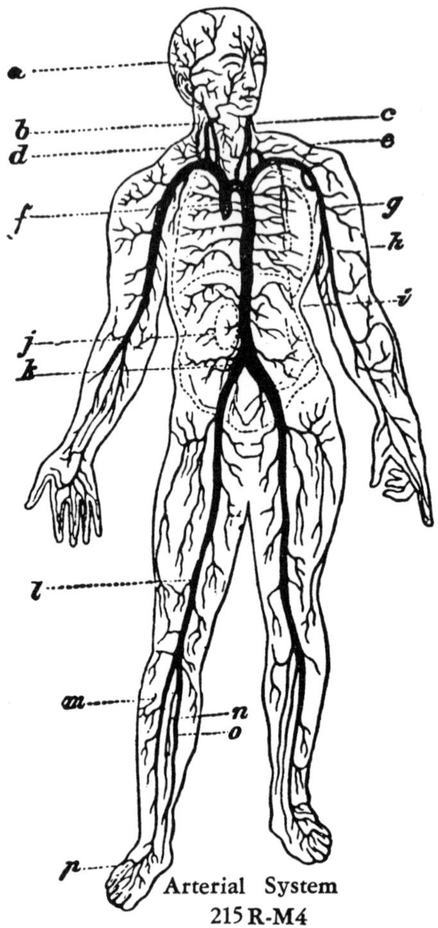

Arterial System
215 R-M4

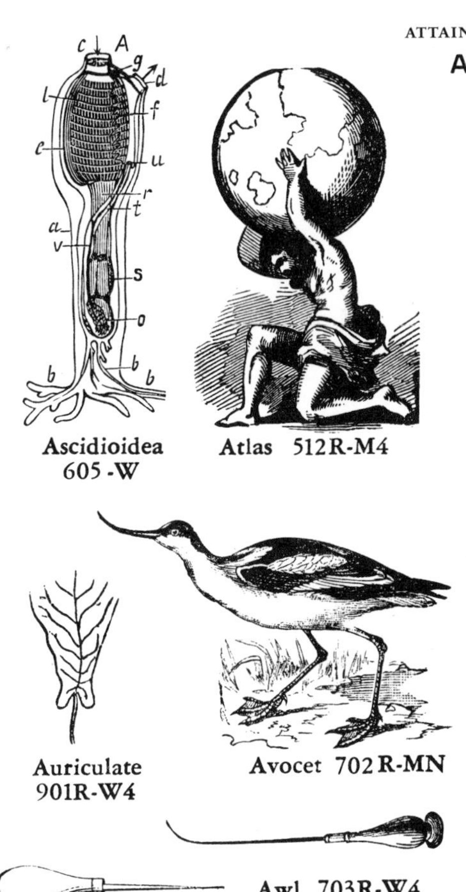

Ascidioidea
605 -W

Atlas 512R-M4

Auriculate
901R-W4

Avocet 702R-MN

Awl 703R-W4

Awl 802-ML

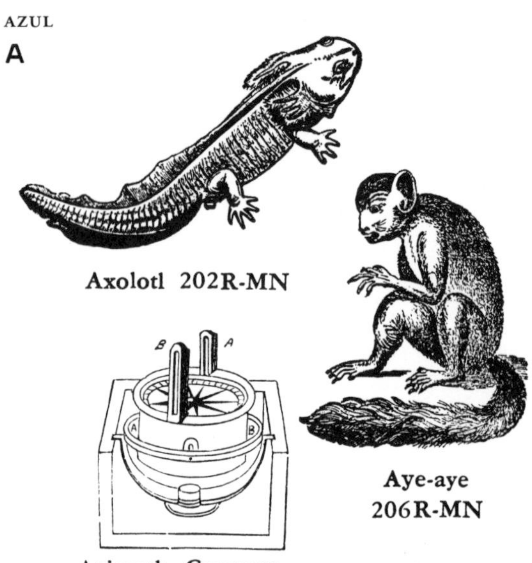

Axolotl 202R-MN

Aye-aye
206R-MN

Azimuth Compass
304R-W4

B

Banana
11 **R-W4**

Banjo
100 **R-ML**

B

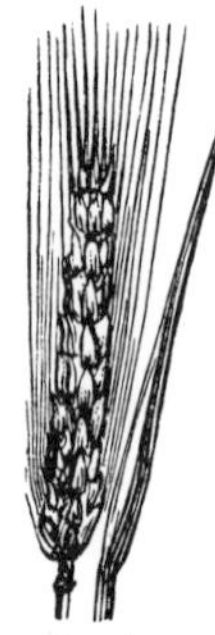

Barley
101 R-W4

Baron's Coronet
1000 R-W4

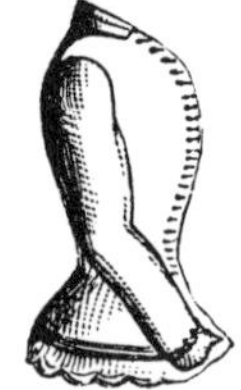

Basque
1001R-W4

Barn Owl
111R-WN

Bee Fly
1100R-MN

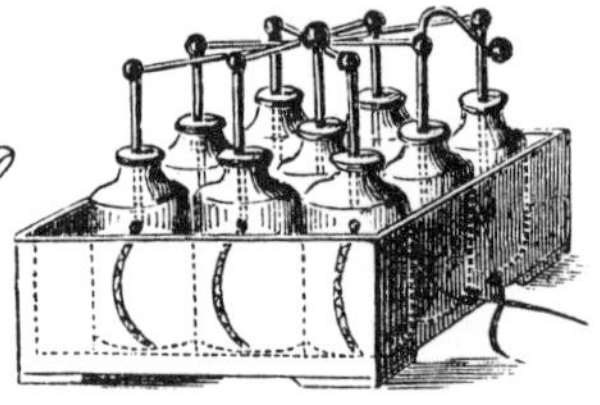

Battery of Leyden Jars
1011R-W4

Barque 1010- D4

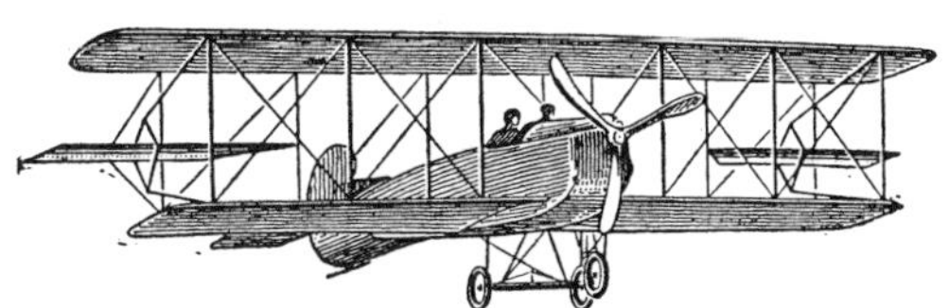

Biplane 11001-M

Bicycle 10010 R-WN

B

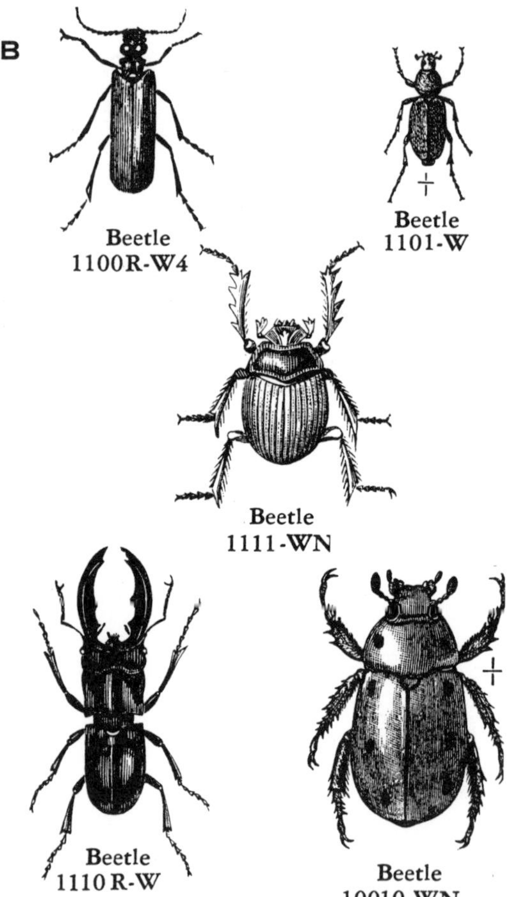

Beetle
1100R-W4

Beetle
1101-W

Beetle
1111-WN

Beetle
1110R-W

Beetle
10010-WN

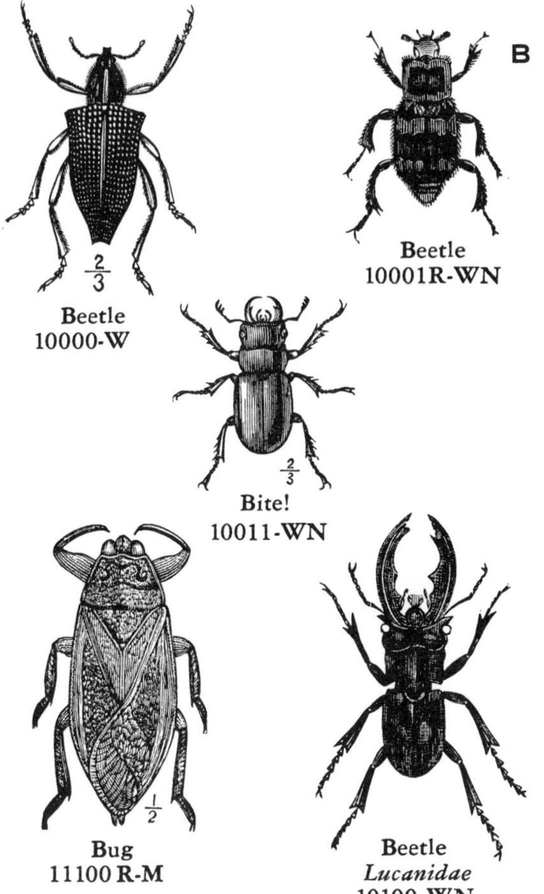

Beetle
10000-W

Beetle
10001R-WN

Bite!
10011-WN

Bug
11100 R-M

Beetle
Lucanidae
10100-WN

B

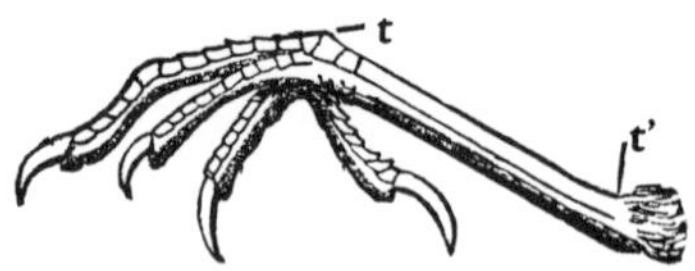

Booted Tarsus (t to t')
11000-MN

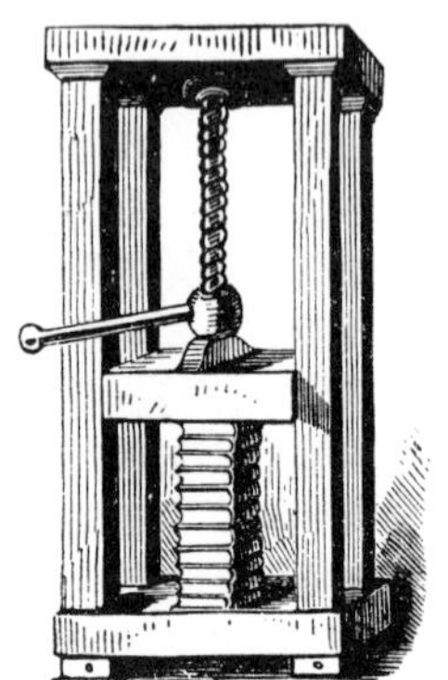

Book Press
10111R-W4

Bolt 10110R-MN

Burin 11101-W4

Bell Jar
10101-WN

Buddha
11011R-M

1

2

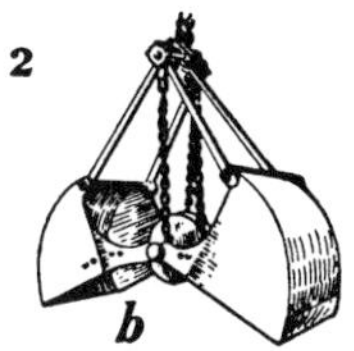

a *b*

Buckets 11001-M

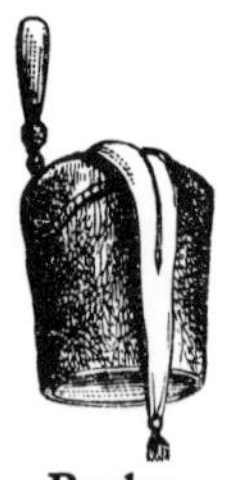

Busby
11111R-W4

Bust 00000R-WI

C

Cam
43-WN

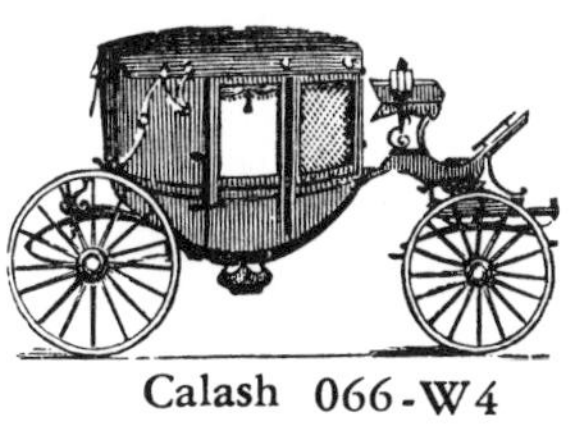

Calash 066-W4

Cam
41D8-W1

Caster
6110-W4

Carrion Crow 109N-WN

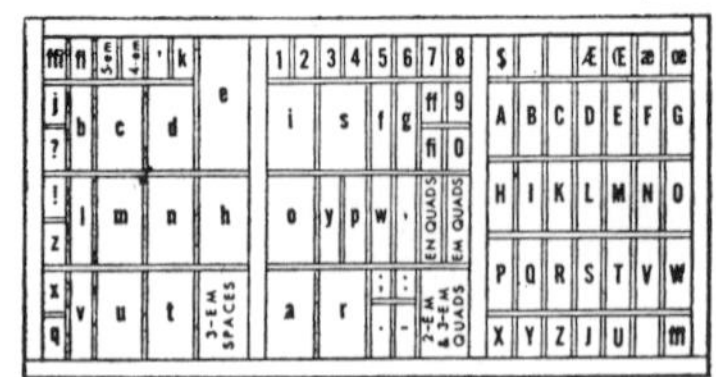

California Type Case 720R-M

Cestus 104-W4

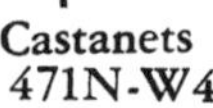

Castanets 471N-W4

Caryatid 43-W4

Capuchin 41-WN (*Cebus capucinus*)

C

Chain Fall
R120-M

Cirrose Leaf
20-W4

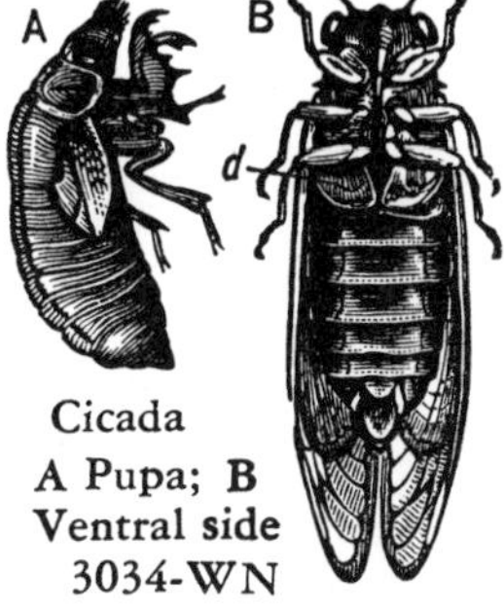

Cicada
A Pupa; B
Ventral side
3034-WN

Cereus (*C. gicanteus*)
& Indians 20R-MN

Ceres
Q1D7-W4

C

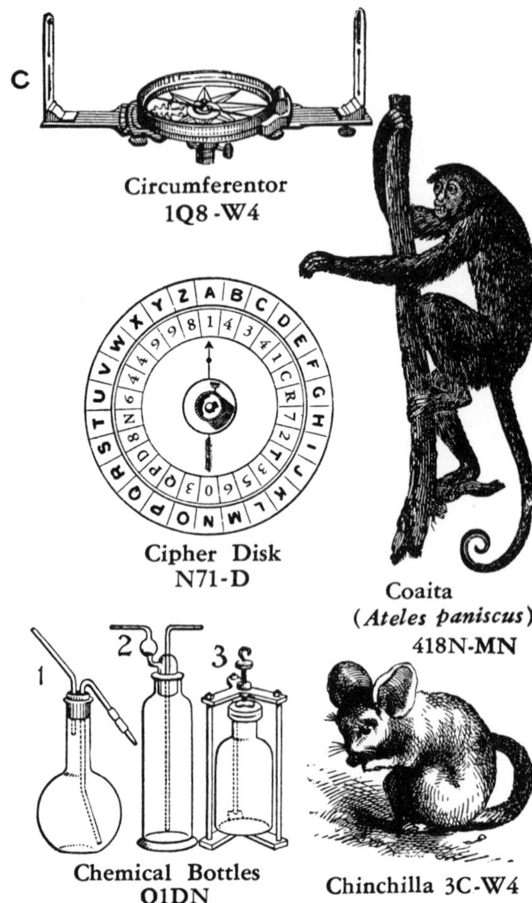

Circumferentor
1Q8-W4

Cipher Disk
N71-D

Coaita
(*Ateles paniscus*)
418N-MN

Chemical Bottles
Q1DN

Chinchilla 3C-W4

Clio 103-W4

Close
128-WI

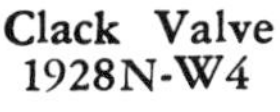

Clack Valve
1928N-W4

Clepsydra
20-W4

Clarinet 4283-MN

Cleat 341D9-MN

C

Colliope 4132-MN

Colossus of Rhodes Q71-WI

Collie D20R-MN

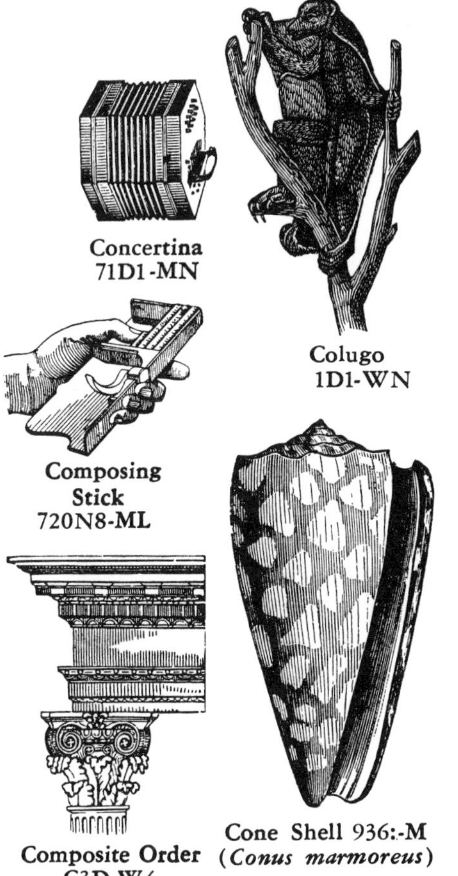

Concertina
71D1-MN

Colugo
1D1-WN

Composing
Stick
720N8-ML

Composite Order
C3D-W4

Cone Shell 936:-M
(*Conus marmoreus*)

C

Cormorant (*Carbo cormoramus*) 438N-W4

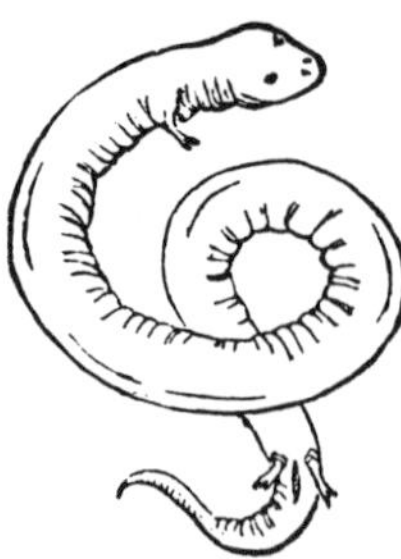

Congo Snake 308Q-MN

Conoid 3DN8-M4

Counter 51R-M

Cone of Pine 1048-MN

Compsognathus 5203-MN

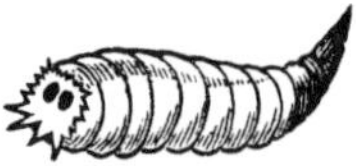

Corn Fly Larva N9Q-MN

C

Cockatoo
3RD1-W4

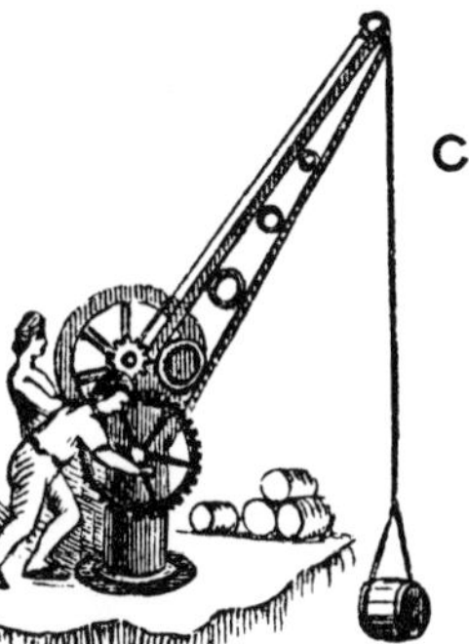

Crane Q79-W4

Counterbalance 155-W4

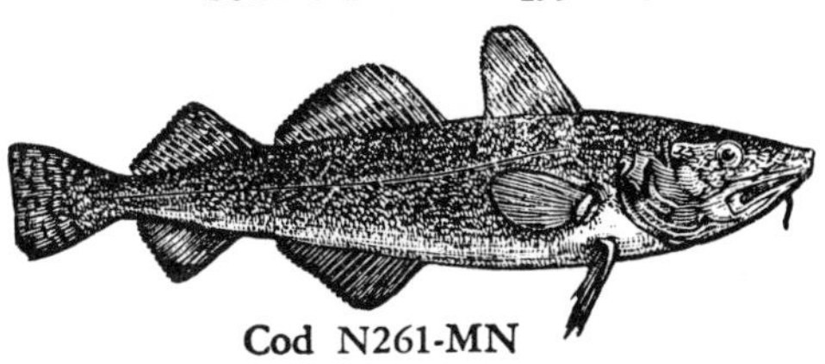

Cod N261-MN

C

Coupe 4181-W4

Croton Bug (*Ectobia Germanica*) 72NN-WN

Coupling 4155-MN

Cog Wheel N43-W4

Copying Press 1D8-W4

Coypu (*Myopotamus coypus*) R35C

Crawfish 336D-W4

Crocodile (*Crocodilus vulgaris*) 818-M

Cusp
20-MN

Cuckoo, Yellow-Billed
(*Coccyzus Americanus*)
428N-MN

Curling Stone
1031-ML

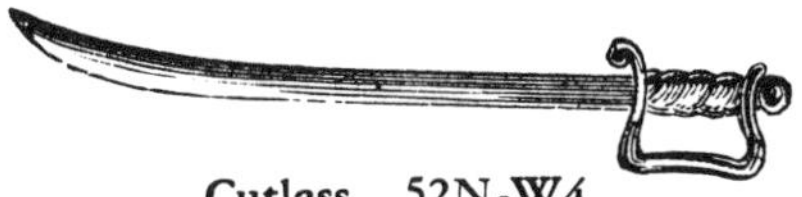

Cutlass 52N-W4

C

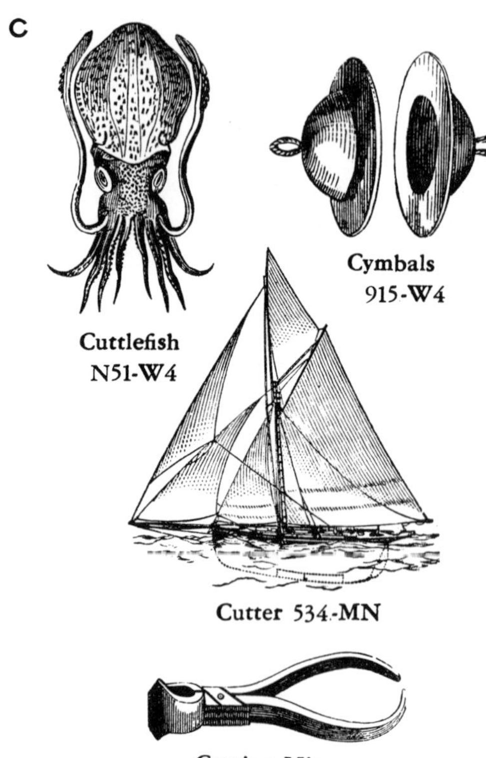

Cuttlefish
N51-W4

Cymbals
915-W4

Cutter 534-MN

Cutting Nippers
Q255-WN

D

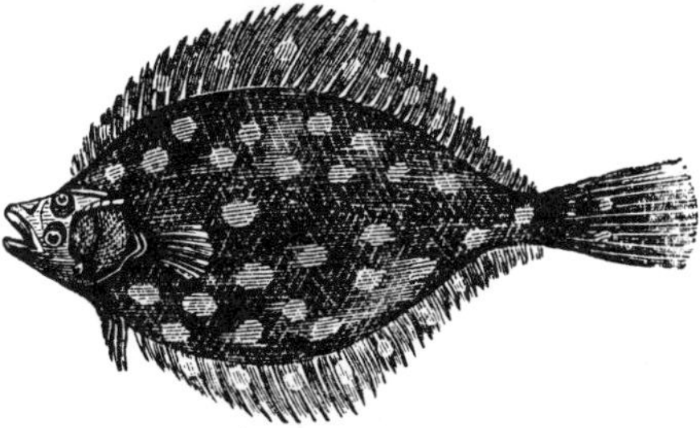

Dab 22R-M

Dachshund 44 R-MN

D

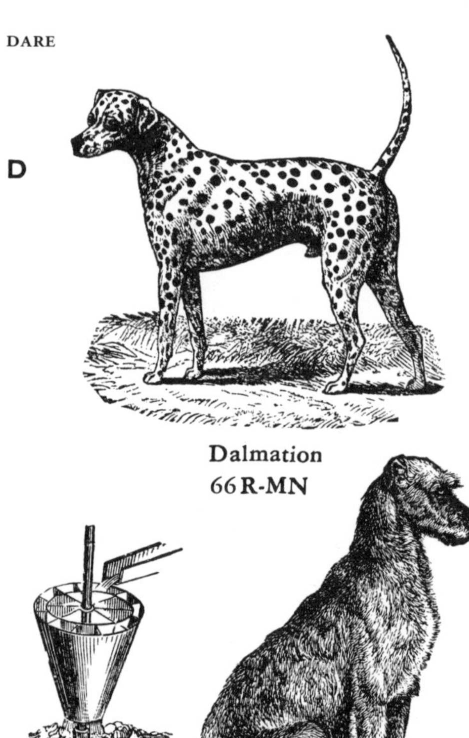

Dalmation
66R-MN

Danaide
88R-WI

$\frac{1}{20}$

Deerhound 110R-MN

Dandie Dinmont 132 R-WN

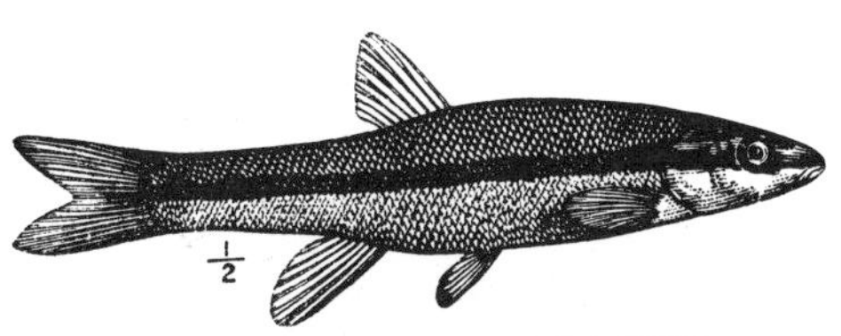

Dace (Black-nosed) 154 -WN
(*Rhinichthys atronasus*)

Daman (*Hyrax syriacus*) 176 R-MN

D

Deadly Nightshade
(*Atropa Belladonna*)
198 R-MN

Decoration
220 R-W4

Danish Dog 242 R-MN

Debruised
264 R-W4

Dehiscent Silicula
286 R-WI

Decompound
308 R-W4

Deer 330-MN

D

Displayed
396 R-WI

Dial of
Timepiece
374-MN

Dentate
352-W4

Dhole 418R-MN

D

Diandrous
440R-W4

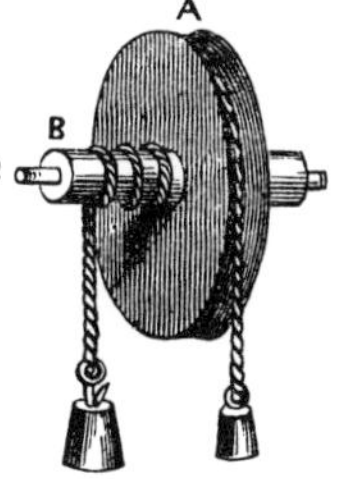

Differential
462R-W9

Dice
484R-W

Diadelphous Stamens
506R-W4

Didelphis (*D. murina*)
528R-MN

D

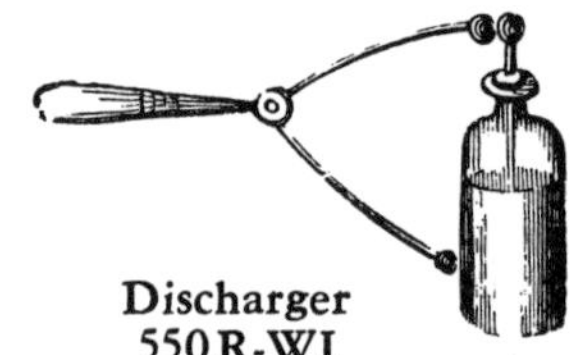

Discharger
550R-WI

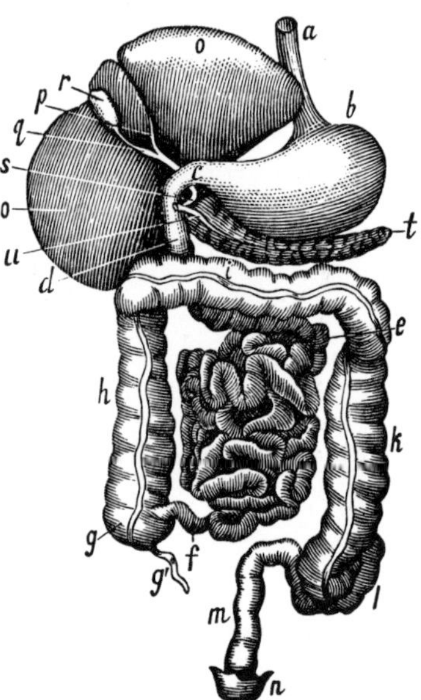

Digestive Apparatus

572R-WN

Disk 594 R-W4
d disk; r,r rays

Dingo (*Canus dingo*)
616 R-MN

Diodon
638R-W4

Diver 660R-W4

DOVETAIL

D

Dormant
682 R-WI

Dog 704-MN

Doris 726 R-MN

E

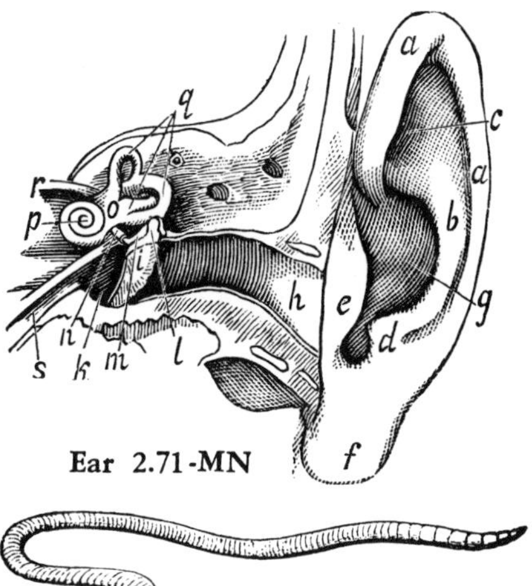

Ear 2.71-MN

Earthworm 828-M

E

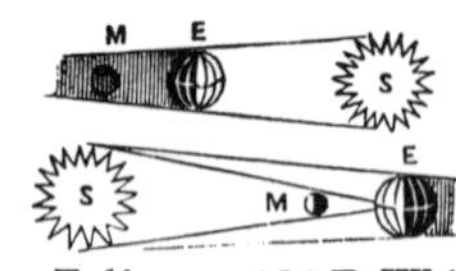

Eclipse 182 R-W4

Eared Owl (*Asio otus*) 590-WN

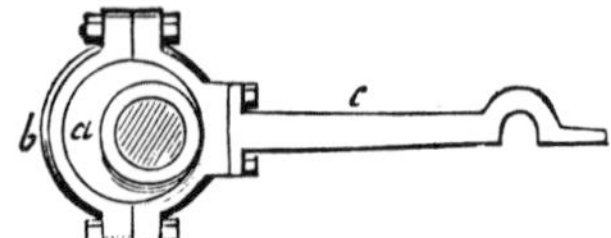

Eccentric 84 R-MN

Echinate 45 R-W4

Echidna (*E. hystrix*) 235 R-MN

Edelweiss
287R-MN

E

Edentate
360R-MN
(*Cyclothurus didactylus*)

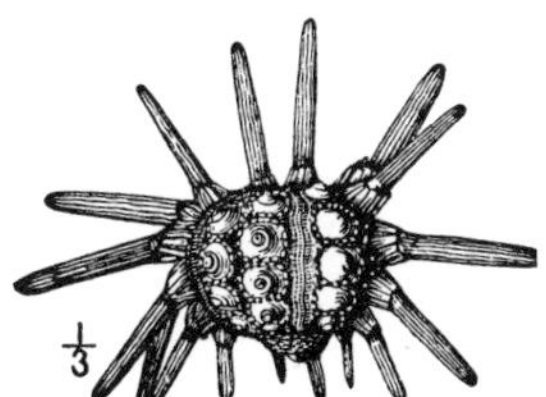

Echinoidea 471.-WN
(*Phyllacanthus dubia*)

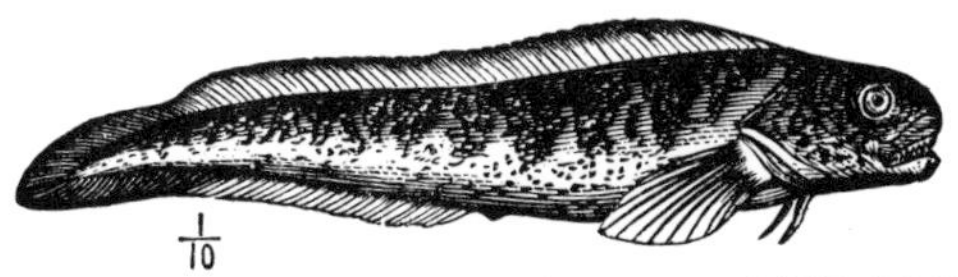

Eelpout (*Zoarces viviparus*) 352R-MN

E

Egret 662-WN
(*Ardea garzetta*)

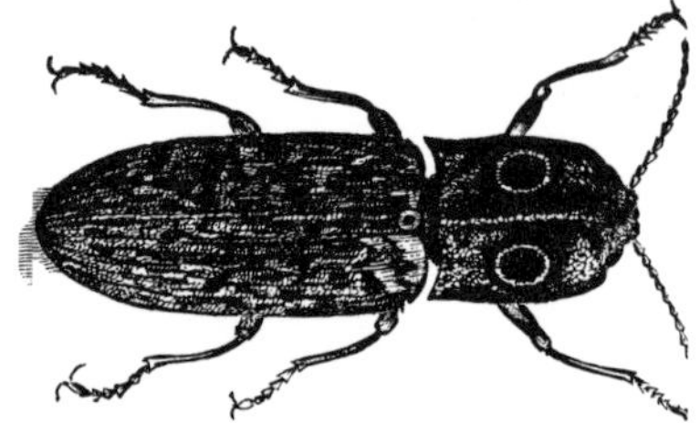

Elater (*E. oculatus*) 497R-MN

Eland (*Taurotragus*) 75R-MN

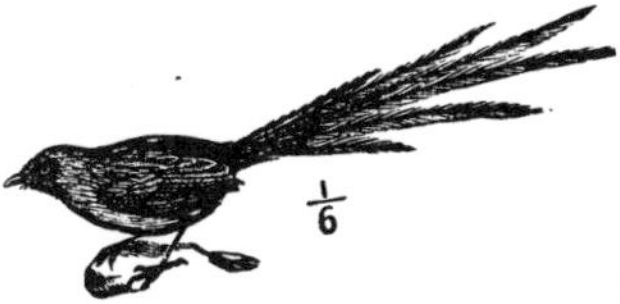

$\frac{1}{6}$

E

Emu Wren 72R-MN
(*Stipiturus malachurus*)

$\frac{1}{50}$

Embossed
93R-WN

Emu 470R-MN
(*Dromaius Novae-Hollandiae*)

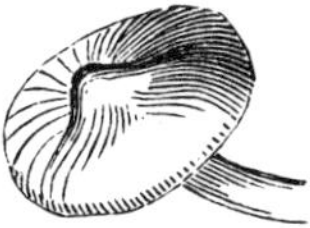

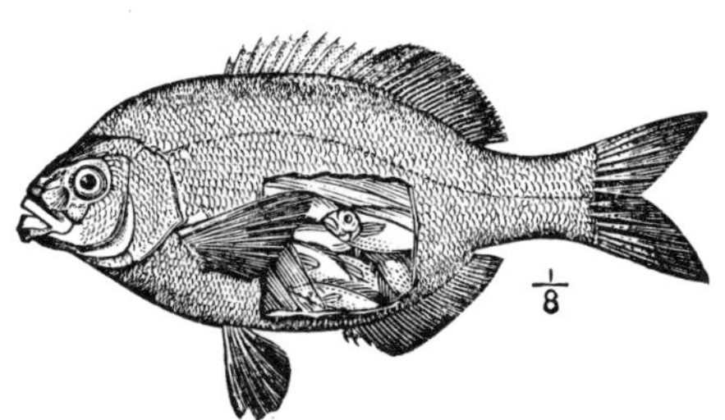

$\frac{1}{8}$

Embiotocoid 69R-MN

E

Elephant 14225-DI

Epaulet
1089R-W4

Eider (*Somateria* sp.) 1331R-MN

Engine Lathe 669R-WN

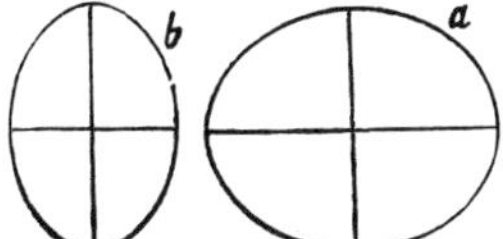

Ellipsoidal Plane Sections
676R-W

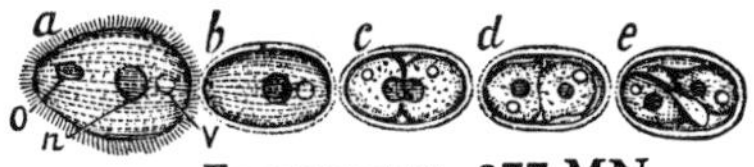

Encystment 277-MN

Erd Shrew
(*Sorex vulgaris*)
2407R-MN

Ermine 6630R-MN
(*Mustela erminea*)

E

Erased
353-WI

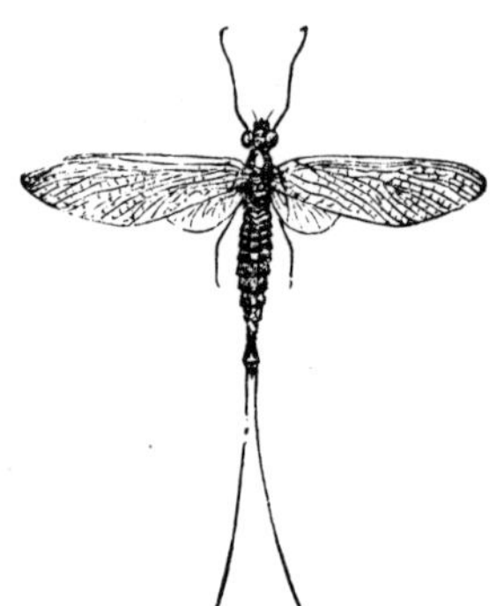

Ephemeral Fly 547R-MN

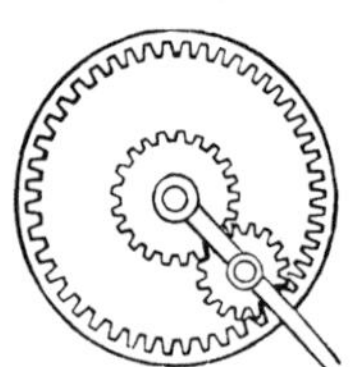

Epicyclic train
594-WN

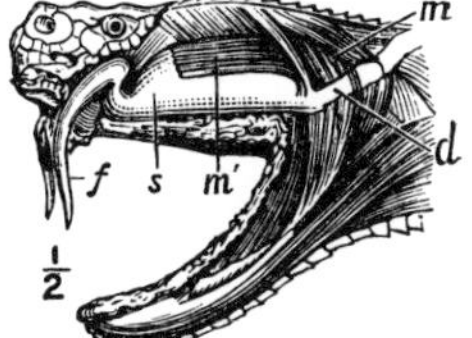

Fangs 2-WN

Fan Training 3-W4

F

Fandango 5R-W4

Feather
8-WN

Fern
(Lady Fern)
13R-M4

Fez 21-WN

Flag of the United States of America 34-W

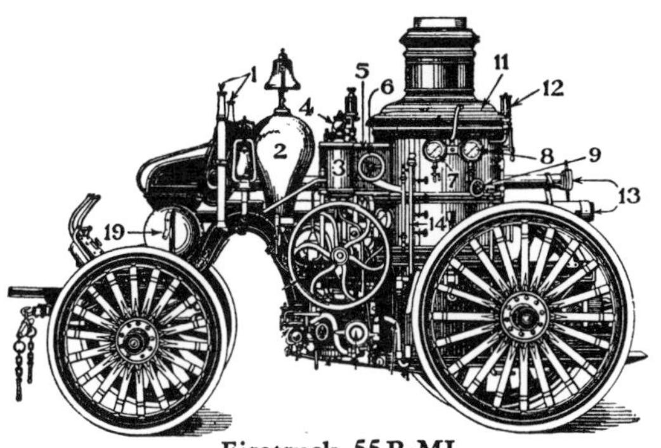

Firetruck 55R-ML

F

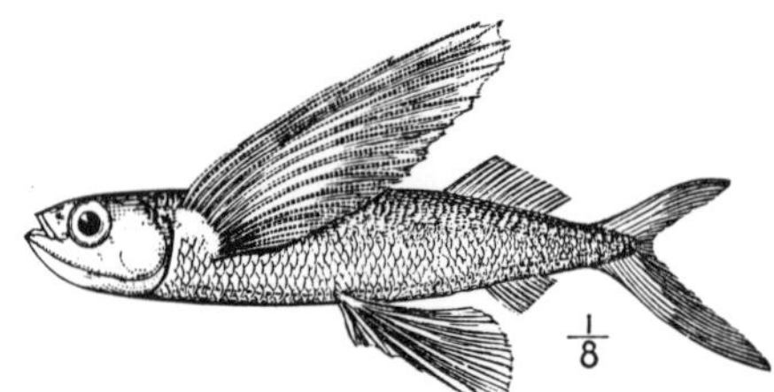

Flying Fish 89-MN

Frogfish 144R-MN
(*Pterophrynoides histrio*)

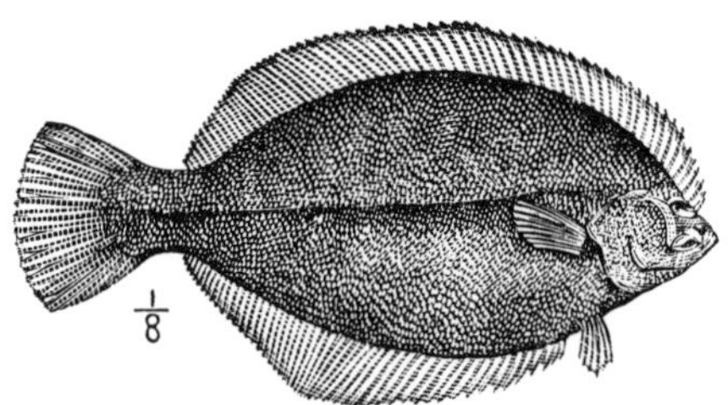

Flat Fish 233-WN

F

Flying Gurnard 377-WN
(*Cephalacanthus volitans*)

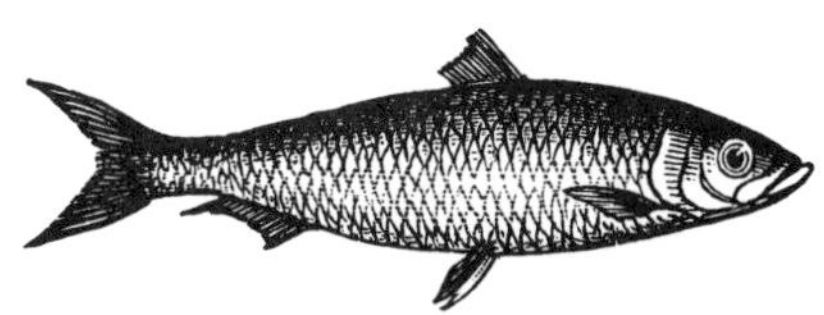

Flunkfish 610-M

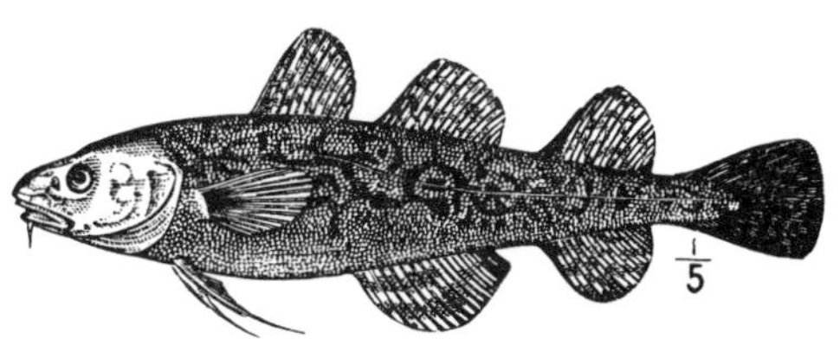

Frostfish 987-WN
(*Microgadus tomcod*)

F

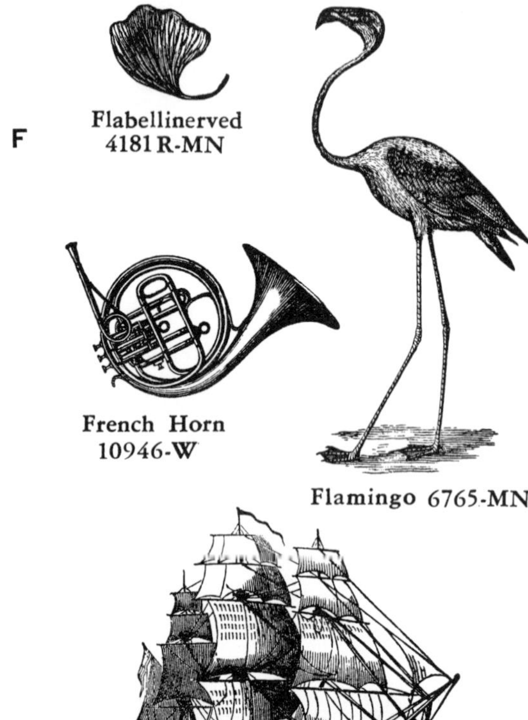

Flabellinerved
4181 R-MN

French Horn
10946-W

Flamingo 6765-MN

Frigate (1800-1840) 17711R-M4

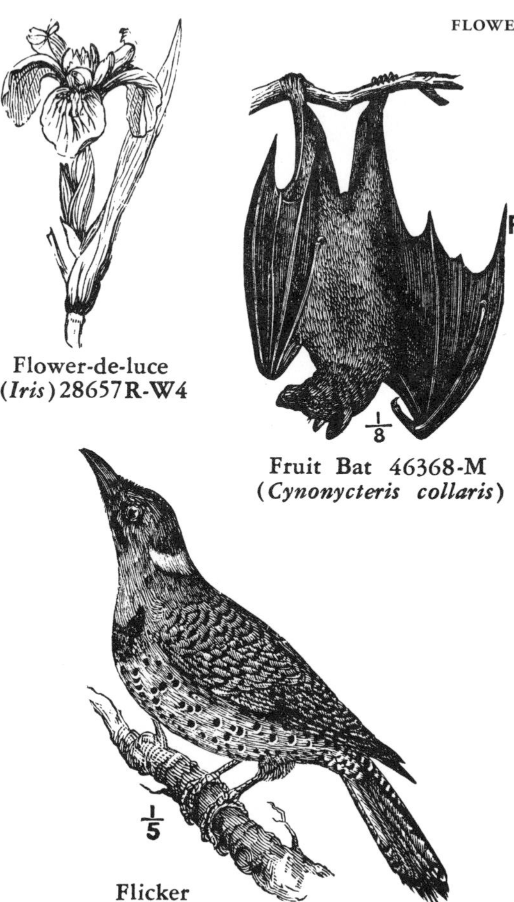

Flower-de-luce
(*Iris*) 28657R-W4

Fruit Bat 46368-M
(*Cynonycteris collaris*)

Flicker
(*Colaptes auratus*) 75025-MN

F

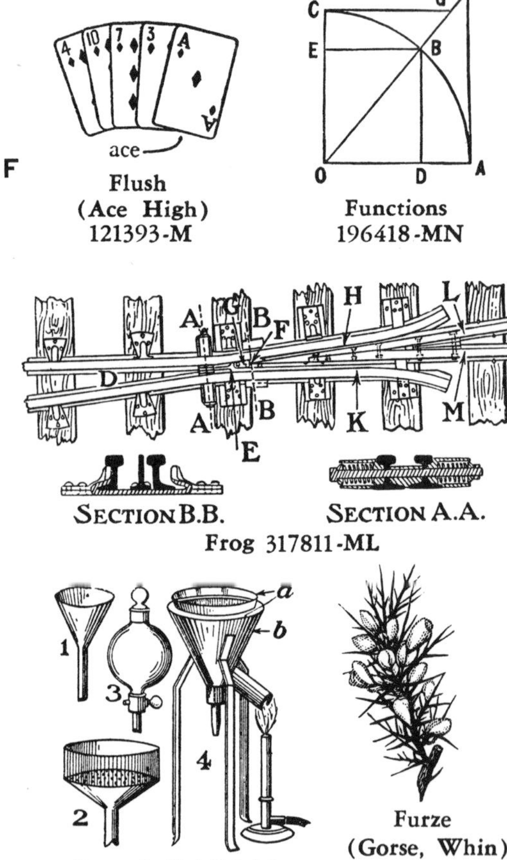

Flush
(Ace High)
121393-M

Functions
196418-MN

SECTION B.B.
SECTION A.A.
Frog 317811-ML

Funnels 514229-M

Furze
(Gorse, Whin)
832040-WN

G

Gaiter 455R-W4

Gabion 575R-W

Gadfly (*Hypoderma bovis*)
350-MN

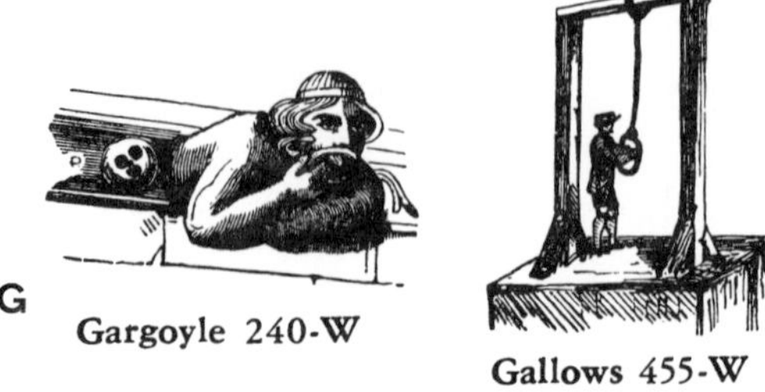

G

Gargoyle 240-W

Gallows 455-W

Gapeworm 180 R-MN

Gazelle 450R-MN
(*Gazella dorcas*)

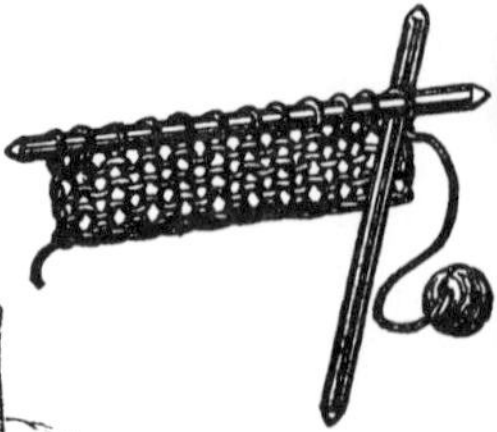

Garter Stitch
570 R-M

Gauntlet
460R-W4

Gemsbok 495R-MN
(*Oryx capensis*)

Geometrid (Larva)
(*Zerene catenaria*)
505 R-MN

Gentian 155-WN
(*Gentiana verna*)

Geophila 510 R-MN
(*Pallifera dorsalis*)

Giraffe 440-WN
(*Camelopardalis giraffa*)

G

Gnu (*Catoblephas gnu*) 530-**MN**

Glockenspiel 170-ML

Gila Monster
(*Heloderma suspectum*)
440 R-MN

Glume
485R-W9

G

1/15

Gibbon (Wou-wou)
(*Hylobates agilis*)
376R-MN

Gocart 502R-W4

Glyptodon 374R-W9
(*Glyptodon clavipes*)

Gondola 327-WN

G

Grass Finch 187-MN
(*Poocaetes gramineus*)

Grain Moth
(*Tinea granella*)
500 R-MN

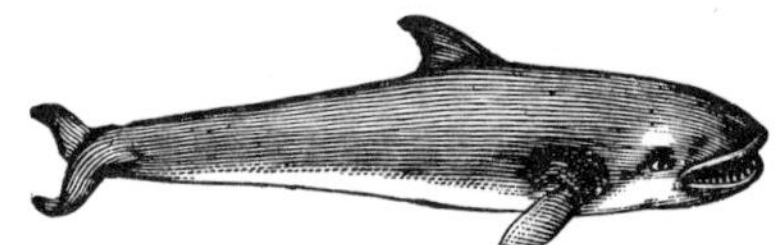

Grampus 106 R-MN

Grallatory 416R-W9
b b Head and Foot of Crane
c c Head and Foot of Stork

Grecian Sphinx
462-W4

Griffin
430R-W4

Greyhound 373R-W4

Grasshopper 201R-MN
(*Caloptenus spretus*)

G

Guillotine
393 **R-W**

Gynandrous
572 **R-W4**

Gonozooid
396-**WN**

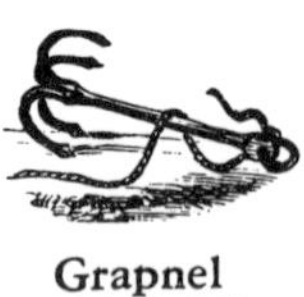

Grapnel
401R-W

Guitar
178 R-W

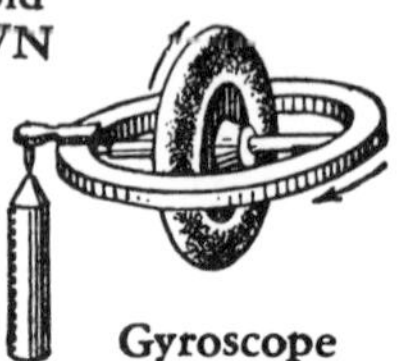

Gyroscope
543 **R-ML**

Hadley's Quadrant
7R-W4

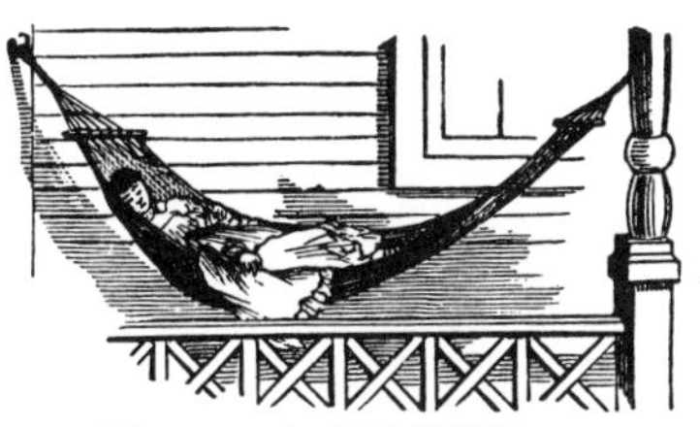

Hammock 13R-WN

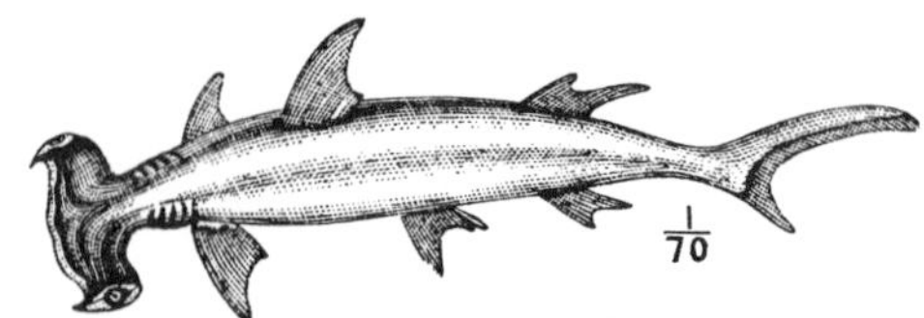

Hammerhead Shark 19-WN
(*Sphyrna tudes*)

H

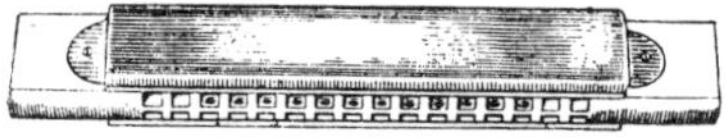

Harmonica 23 R-M

Hammerlock 79-ML

Half notes
31 R-M

Halberd
97 R-W

Hamster 103 R-WN
(*Cricetus frumentarius*)

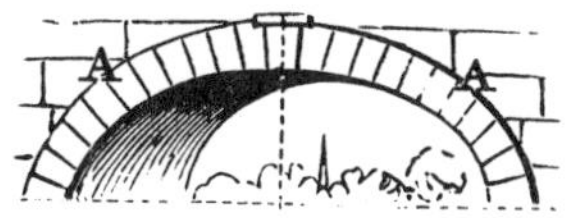

Haunches of Arch
109R-W4

Hauberk
139 R-W4

Hurdy-Gurdy 167-DI

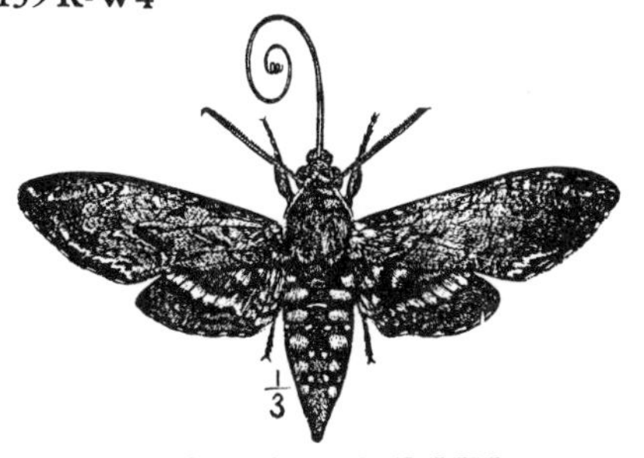

Hawkmoth 193R-MN
(*Macrosila carolina*)

H

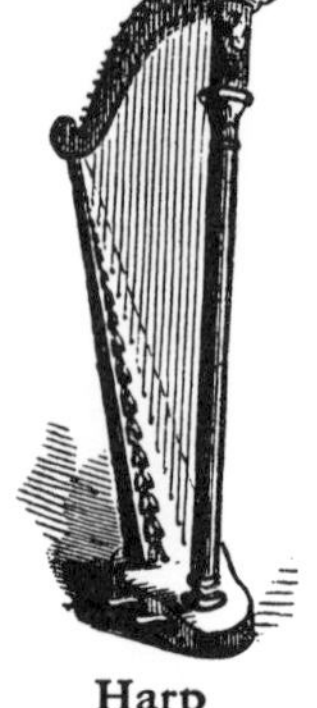

Harp
239 R-W4

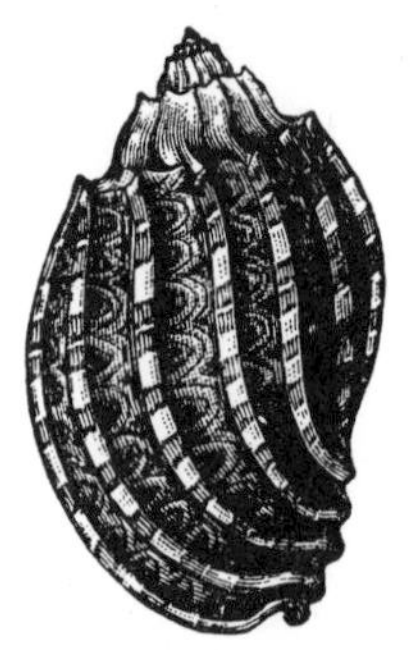

Harp Shell
263R-MN
(*Harpa articularis*)

Heartshaped
293 R-W

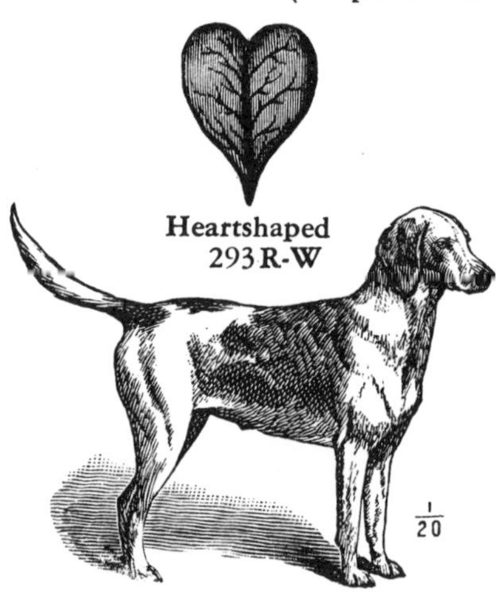

Harrier 313R-MN

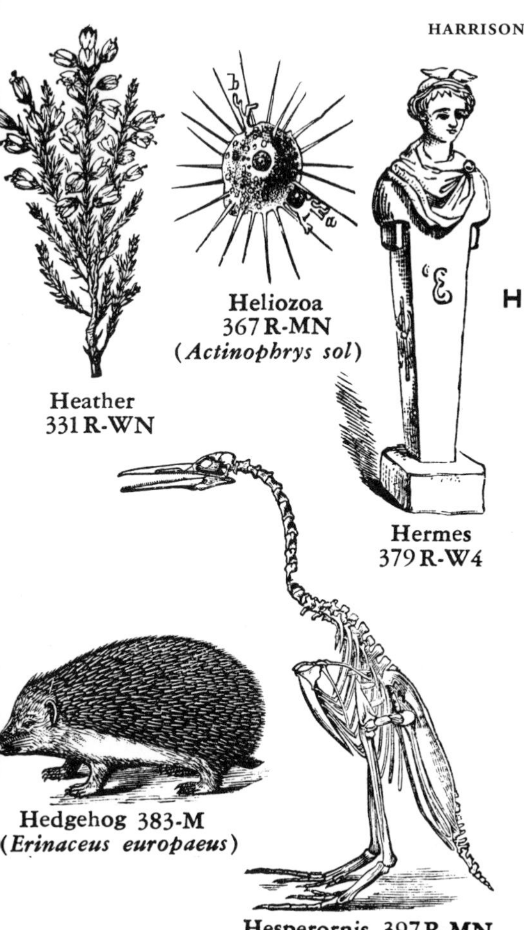

Heather
331 R-WN

Heliozoa
367 R-MN
(*Actinophrys sol*)

Hermes
379 R-W4

H

Hedgehog 383-M
(*Erinaceus europaeus*)

Hesperornis 397 R-MN

Heteropoda 409-WN

H

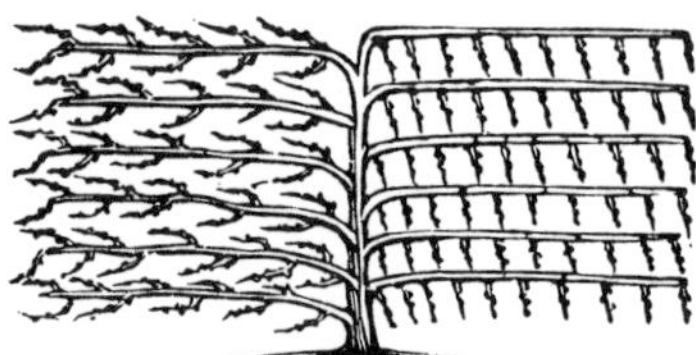

Horizontal Training 487 R-W4

Honey Bee
617R2-M

Heron 563R-W4
(*Ardea cinerea*)

Holothurioidea 653-WN

Horn of the Hunter
673-W4

Hop 683R-W4
(*Humulus lupulus*)

Horned Owl 709R-MN
(*Bubo virginianus*)

H

Hourglass
739R-W4

Hornbill 761-W4

Hyena 863R-MN

Hydrostatic Balance
881R-W4

Ichneumon Fly
66-MN

Ibis 90-MN
(*Ibis aethiopica*)

$\frac{1}{20}$

Ichneumon
80-MN

Ice Skate 15-W

Increscent
395R-WI

Imbricate
95-W4

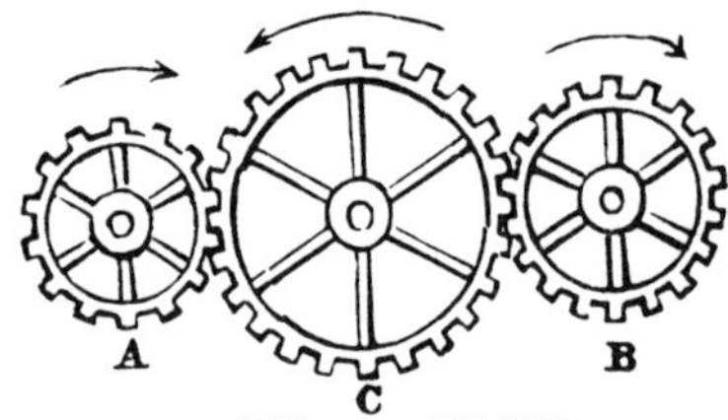

c Idle Wheel 495-W9

Impalement
270-MN

I

Inflamed
40-WI

Inarching
70-W4

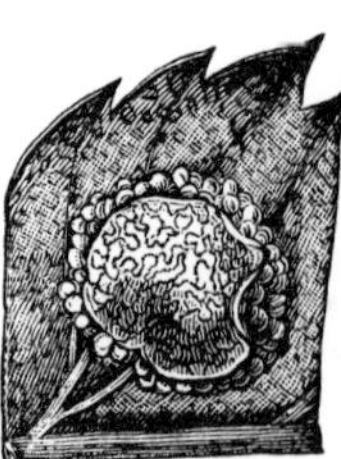

Indusium
295-MN

Inescutcheon
89-W9

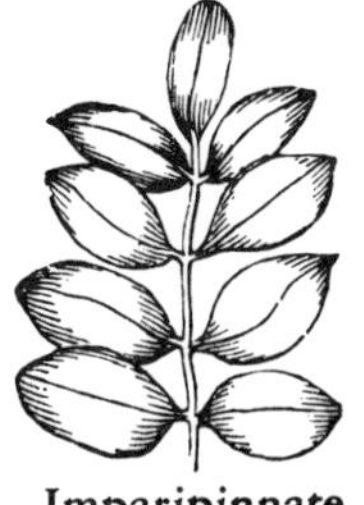

Imparipinnate
695-W4

Interfretted
93-W4

I

Iceland Moss
(*Cetraria islandica*)
25-WN

Ibex 29-MN
(*Capra ibex*)

Incised Leaf
84-M4

Impact Drill
65-M

Issuant
35-W4

I

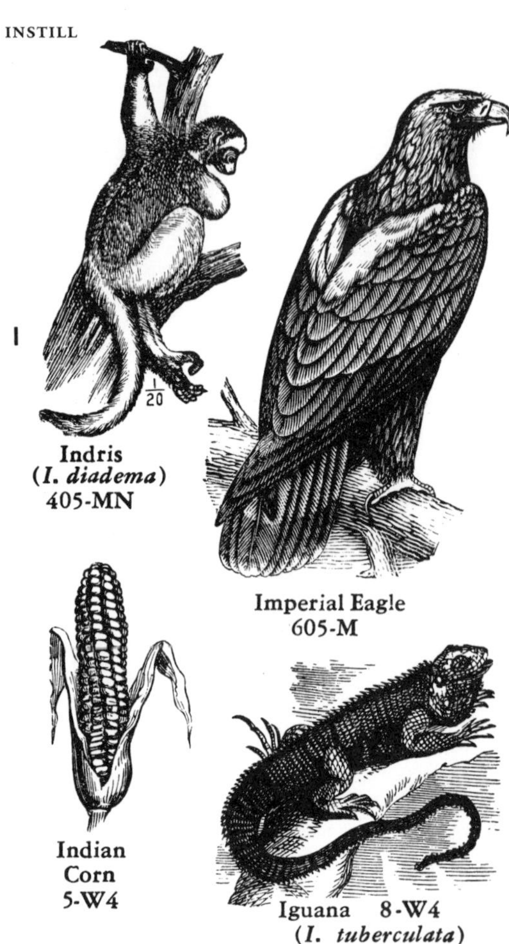

Indris
(*I. diadema*)
405-MN

Imperial Eagle
605-M

Indian
Corn
5-W4

Iguana 8-W4
(*I. tuberculata*)

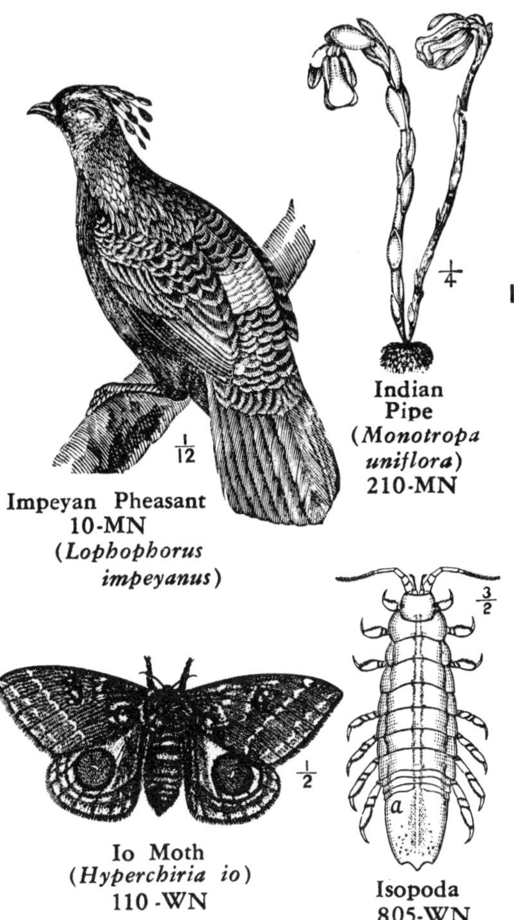

Indian Pipe (*Monotropa uniflora*) 210-MN

Impeyan Pheasant 10-MN (*Lophophorus impeyanus*)

Io Moth (*Hyperchiria io*) 110-WN

Isopoda 805-WN

I

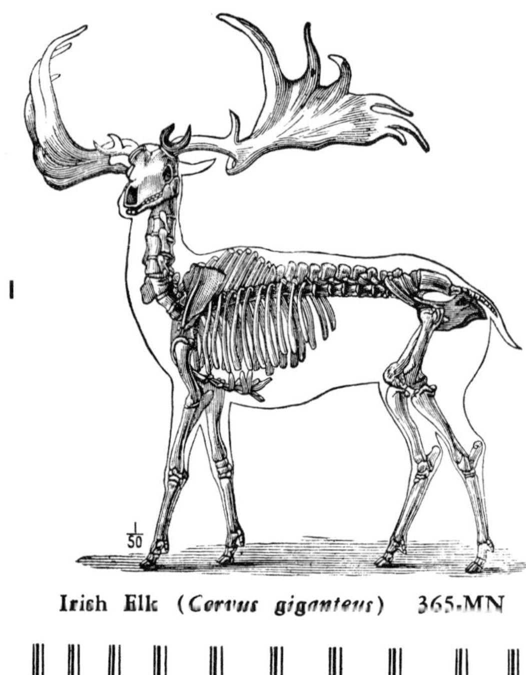

Irish Elk (*Cervus giganteus*) 365-MN

1 2 3 4 5 6 7 8 9 P

Irons 605-M

J

Jaal Goat 77 R-W4
(*Capra jaela*)

Jacamar 5 R-MN
(*Galbula sp.*)

Jabiru
9R-MN
(Saddle-Billed Stork)

Jack
7-ML

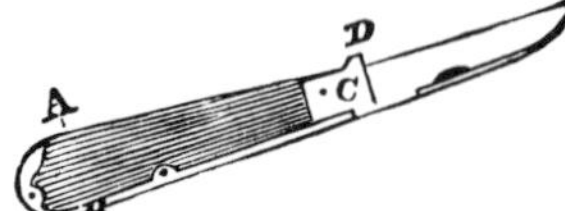

Jackknife 15R-M

J

British Jack
4R-MN

Jackscrew
17-WN

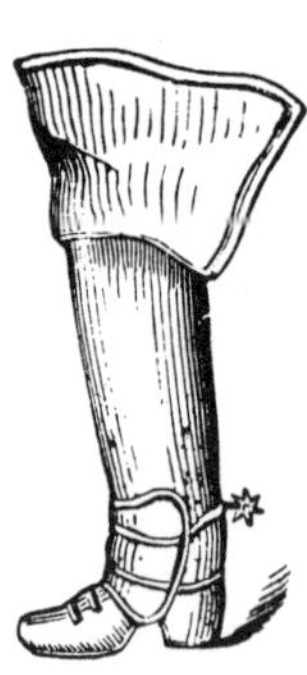

Jack Boot
33R-M4

Jack Plane 2R-W

Jack
8R-M

American Jack
24-W

J

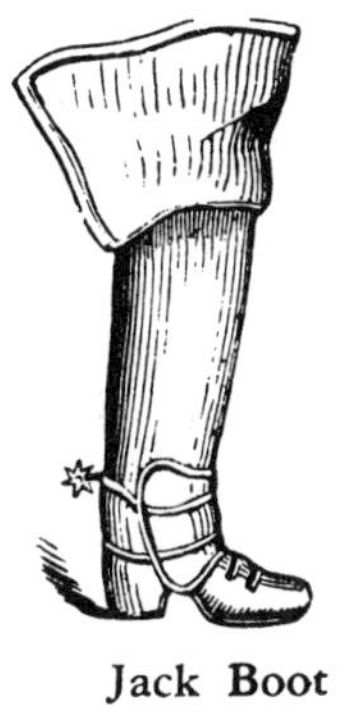

Jack Boot
14R-W4

Jack Coat
18R-MN

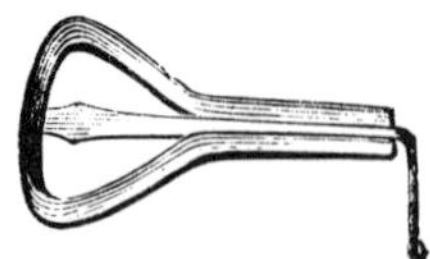

Jaw Harp 15R-MN

Joiner's Gauge
00 R-W

J

Jacksnipe 25R-MN
(*Limnocryptes gallinula*)

Jambes
24-M4

Blue Jay 35R-M

Jigger 22-ML

Jessant
31-WI

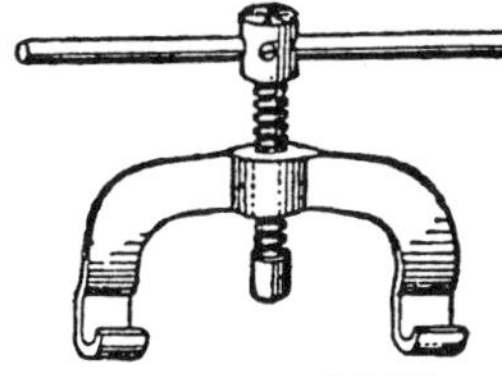
Jim-crow 19-M

J

Jerboa 32R-MN
(*Dipus aegypticus*)

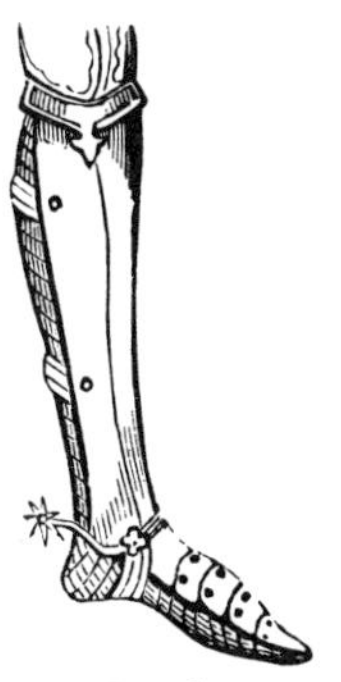
Jambes
3R-W4

J

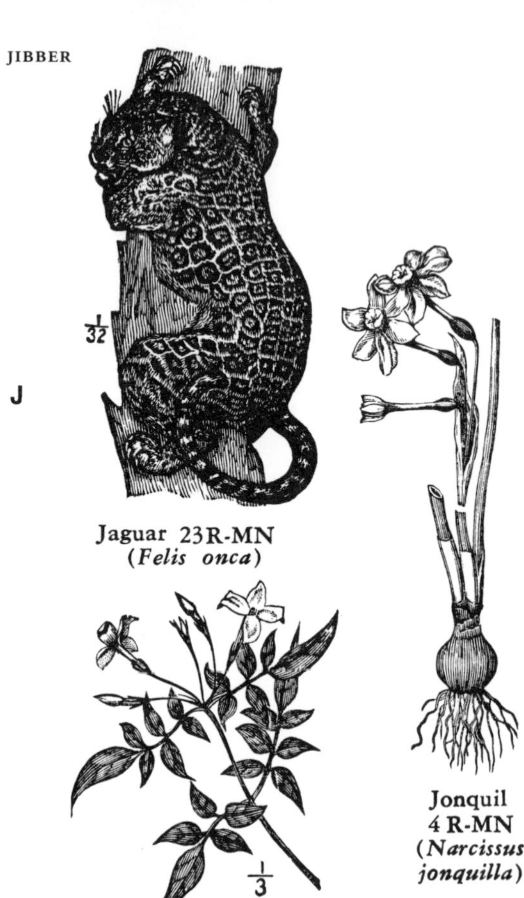

Jaguar 23R-MN
(*Felis onca*)

Jonquil
4 R-MN
(*Narcissus jonquilla*)

Jasmine 6 R-MN
(*Jasmine officinale*)

Jako 1-M

J

Junco (*J. hyemalis*) 27 R-MN

Jump Seat
(One-seat form)
6R-W4

Jump Seat
(Two-seater)
14R-W4

J

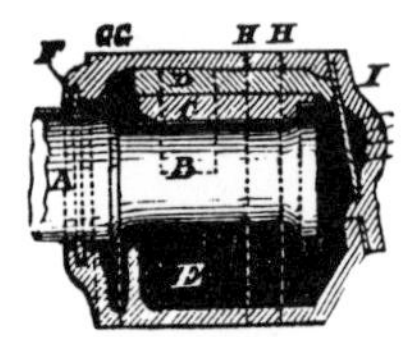

Journal Box
9R-W4

Junk 8R-W

K

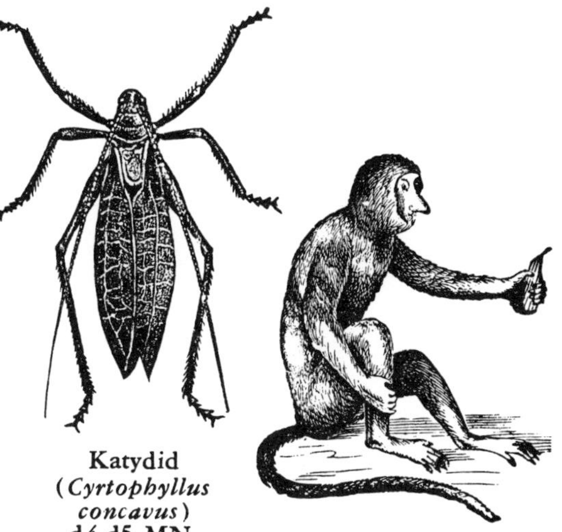

Katydid
(*Cyrtophyllus concavus*)
d4,d5-MN

Kahau Nf3,e6-M
(*Semnopithecus nasalis*)

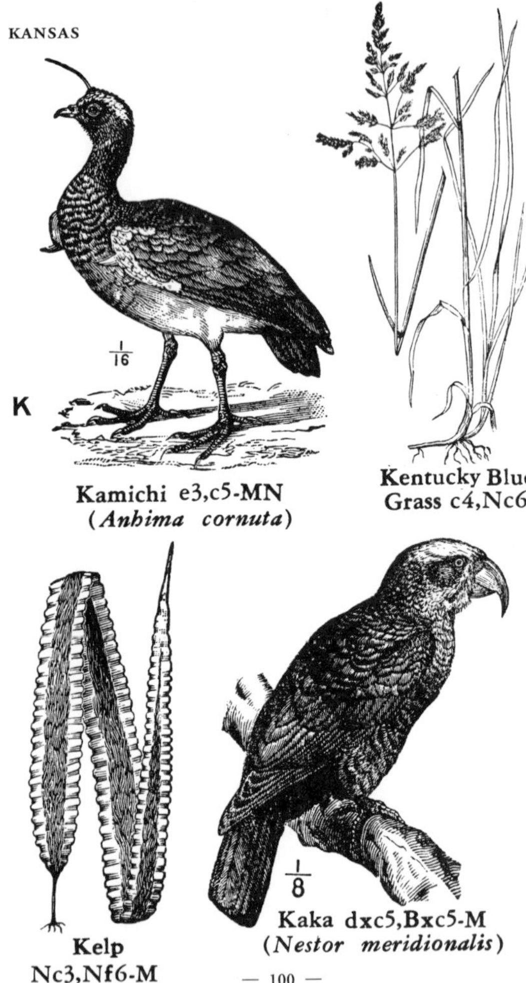

Kamichi e3,c5-MN
(*Anhima cornuta*)

Kentucky Blue Grass c4,Nc6

Kelp
Nc3,Nf6-M

Kaka dxc5,Bxc5-M
(*Nestor meridionalis*)

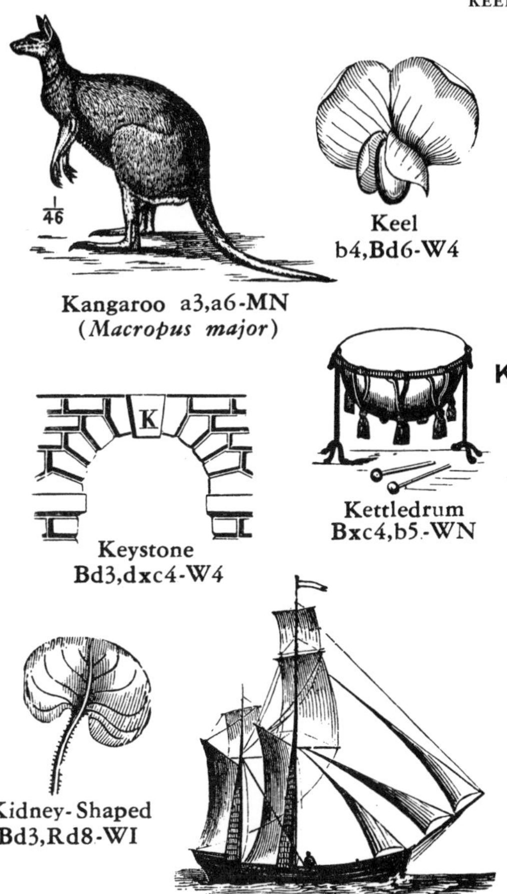

Kangaroo a3,a6-MN
(*Macropus major*)

Keel
b4,Bd6-W4

K

Keystone
Bd3,dxc4-W4

Kettledrum
Bxc4,b5-WN

Kidney-Shaped
Bd3,Rd8-WI

Ketch Qe2,Bb7-W4

Granny
Knot
Nxe5
Bxe5

K

$\frac{1}{7}$

Kingfisher 0-0,Ne5-M

Knight in
Shining Armor
e4,Rac8-W4

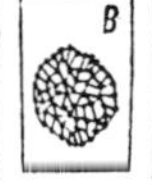

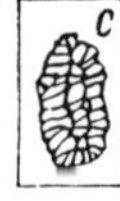

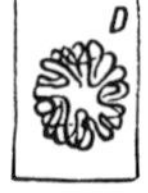

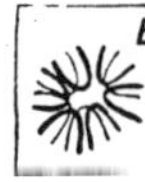

E

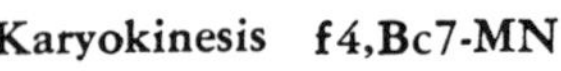

Karyokinesis f4,Bc7-MN

$\frac{1}{120}$

Killer Whale (*Orca gladiator*) e5,Bb6+-W

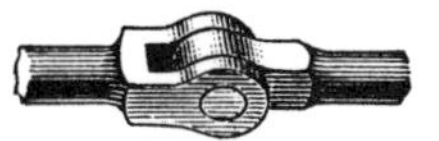

Knuckle Joint
Khl-MN

King Tody
Ng4-MN

Knapsack
g3,Rxc3

King Penguin
Be4,Qh4-M

Square
Knot

K

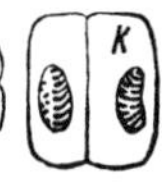

Karyokinesis gxh4,Rd2

Kleeneboc
Qxd2,Bxe4+

K

Koala Qg2-WN
(*Phascolarctos cinereus*)

Kohl-rabi
Rh3-MN

L

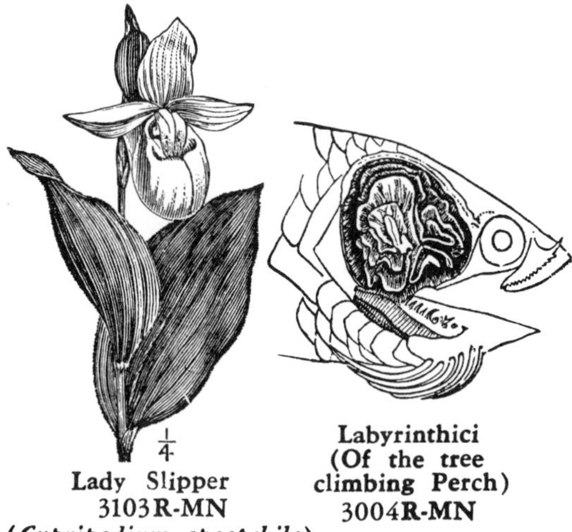

$\frac{1}{4}$

Lady Slipper
3103R-MN
(*Cypripedium spectabile*)

Labyrinthici
(Of the tree
climbing Perch)
3004**R-MN**

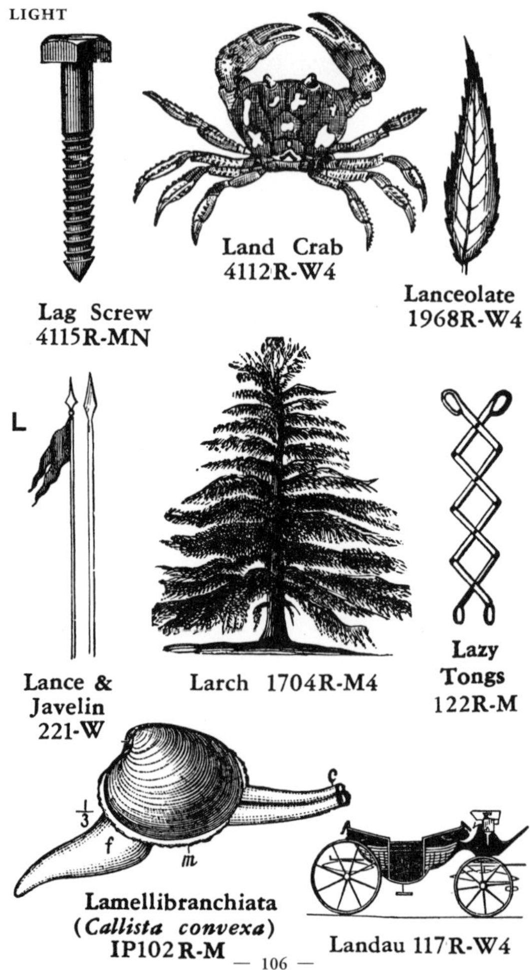

Land Crab
4112R-W4

Lanceolate
1968R-W4

Lag Screw
4115R-MN

Lance &
Javelin
221-W

Larch 1704R-M4

Lazy
Tongs
122R-M

Lamellibranchiata
(*Callista convexa*)
IP102R-M

Landau 117R-W4

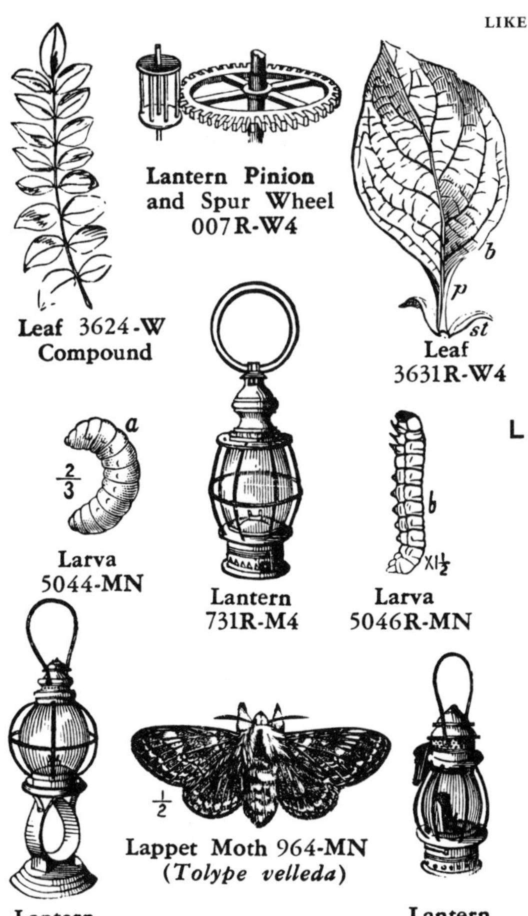

Lantern Pinion and Spur Wheel 007R-W4

Leaf 3624-W Compound

Leaf 3631R-W4

Larva 5044-MN

Lantern 731R-M4

Larva 5046R-MN

Lappet Moth 964-MN (*Tolype velleda*)

Lantern 952R-W4

Lantern 951R-W4

Laughing Jackass
(*Dacelo gigas*) 4833x-MN

L

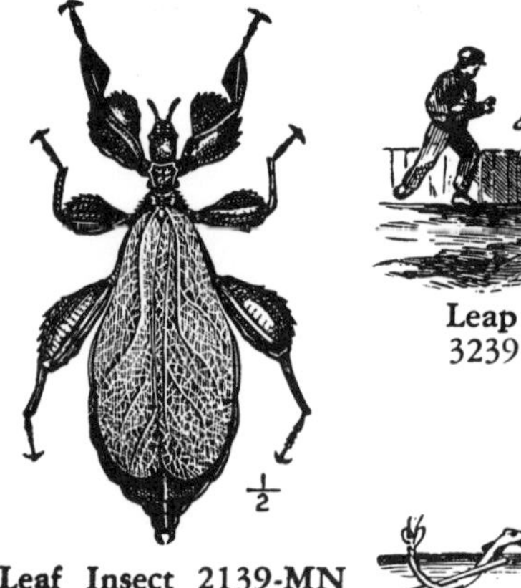

Leap Frog
3239R-W4

Leaf Insect 2139-MN
(*Phyllium siccifolium*)

Layers 0179R-W4

Latitudes 3233-M

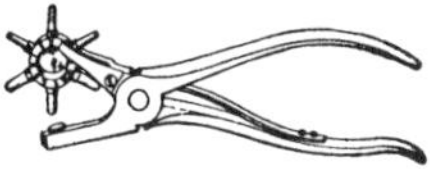

Leather Punch
5476R-M

Laver 308AV-W4

L

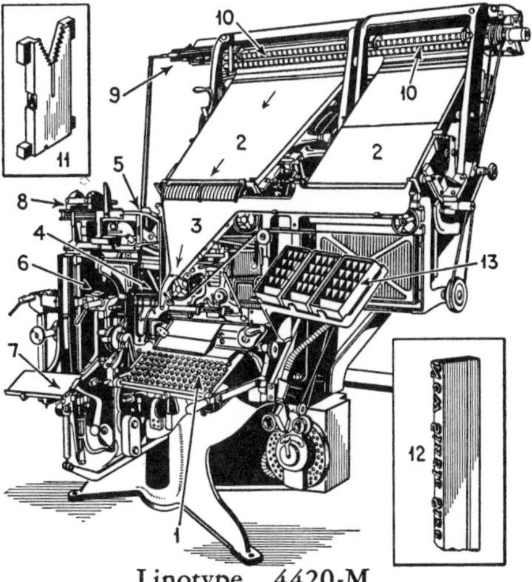

Linotype 4420-M

Leaf Cutter
965R-MN

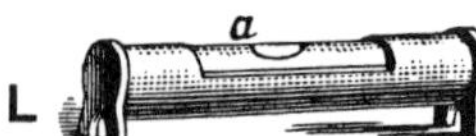

Level 4146-WN

Lemur D12 R-MN
(*Lemur albifrons*)

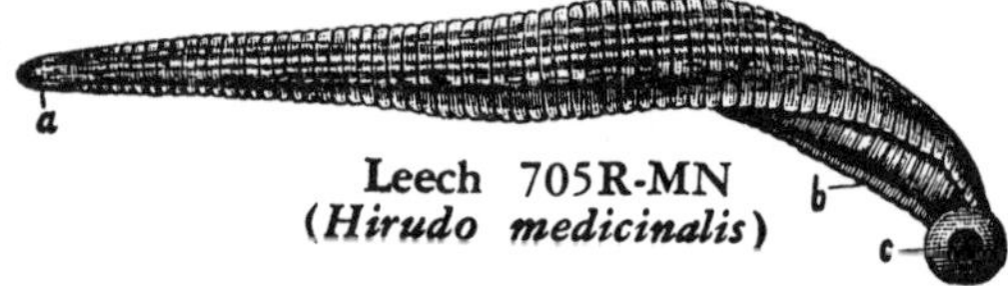

Leech 705R-MN
(*Hirudo medicinalis*)

Letterpress 4117-ML

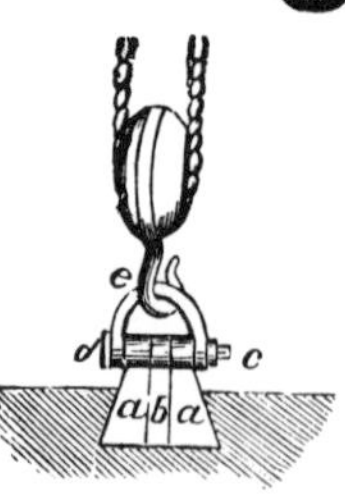

Lewisson
5150R-M4

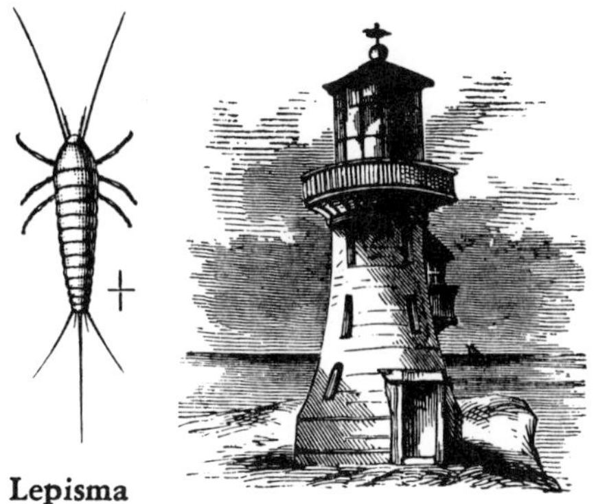

Lepisma
32-WN

Lighthouse C20R-W4

L

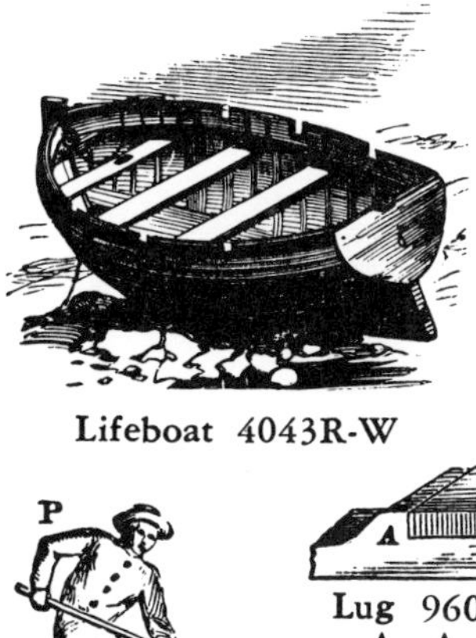

Lifeboat 4043R-W

Lug 960R-W4
A, A Lugs

Lever 3251R-W4

Lingula
(*L. anatina*)
3250R-M

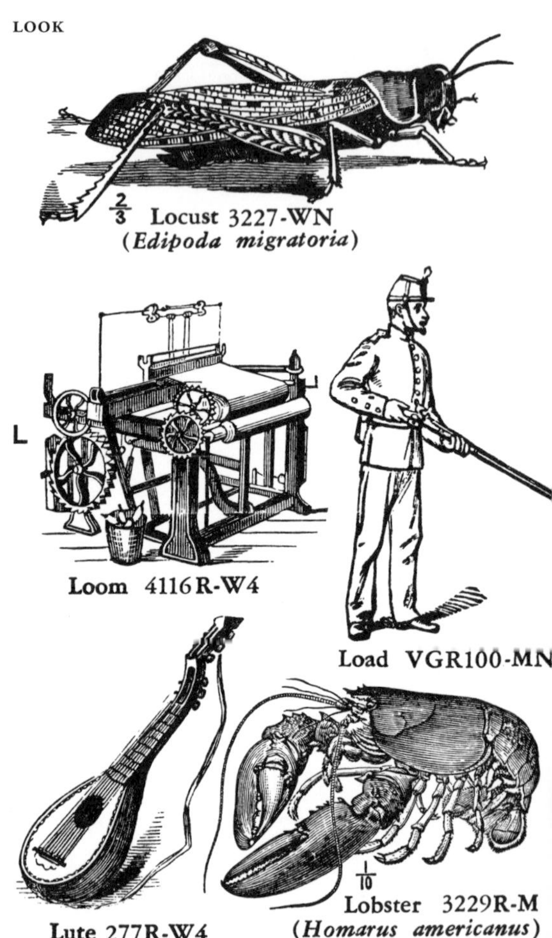

$\frac{2}{3}$ Locust 3227-WN
(*Edipoda migratoria*)

Loom 4116**R-W**4

Load VGR100-**MN**

Lute 277**R-W**4

$\frac{1}{10}$
Lobster 3229**R-M**
(*Homarus americanus*)

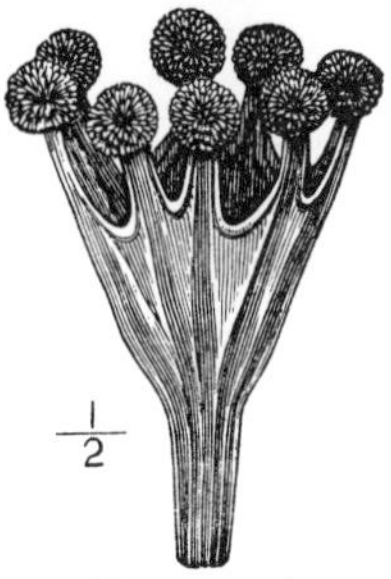

Lucernaria
3234-WN

Lotus 3232R-MN
(*Nelumbium luteum*)

Lugger 123R-W4

Loris 2772-W4

Lynx (*Felis canadensis*) 4415-WN

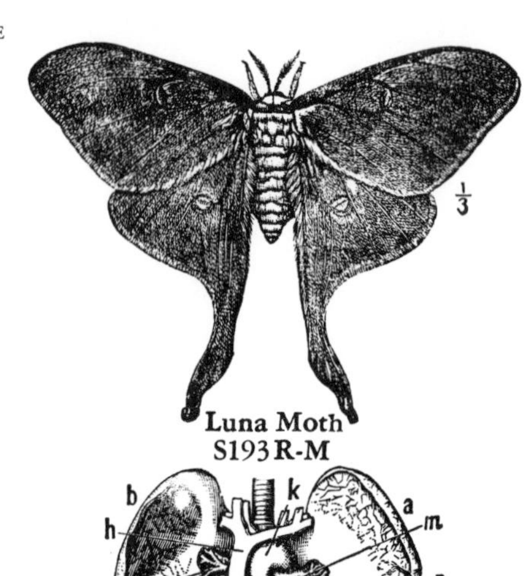

Luna Moth
S193R-M

L

Lungs & Heart
275R-MN

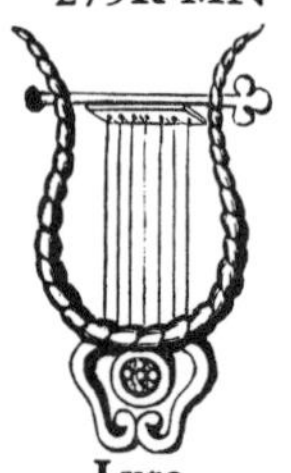

Lyre
543R-W

M

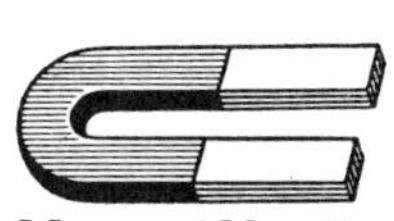

Magnet 183-ML

Maioid Crab 385R-W4
(*Parthenope horrida*)

Maize 425R-MN
(*Zea mays*)

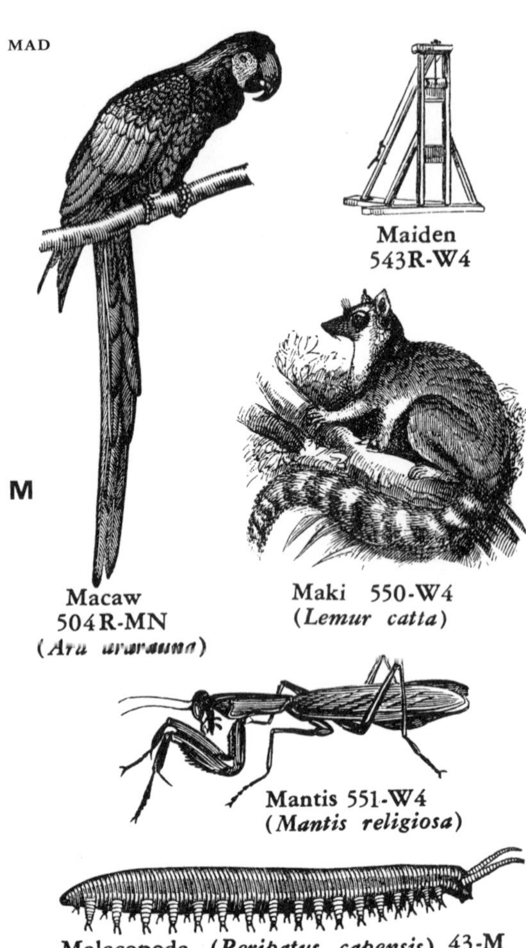

Maiden
543R-W4

M

Maki 550-W4
(*Lemur catta*)

Macaw
504R-MN
(*Ara ararauna*)

Mantis 551-W4
(*Mantis religiosa*)

Malacopoda (*Peripatus capensis*) 43-M

Mandrill 384R-MN
(*Cynocephalus mormon*)

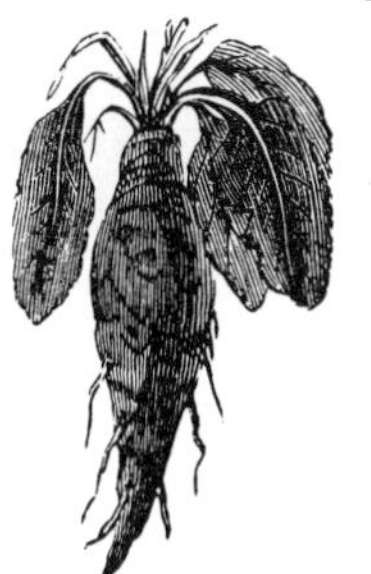

Mangel-Wurzel
48 R-W

Marmoset 87R-MN
(*Midas chrysomelas*)

Manifold 51-WN

M

Mangle
455-M

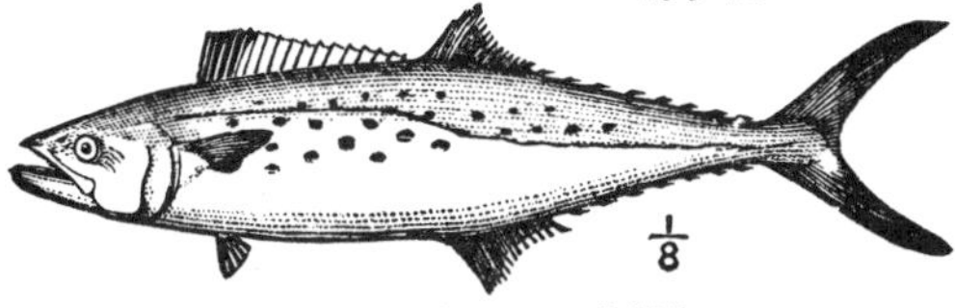

Mackerel 492-MN

Marsh Wren
527R-MN

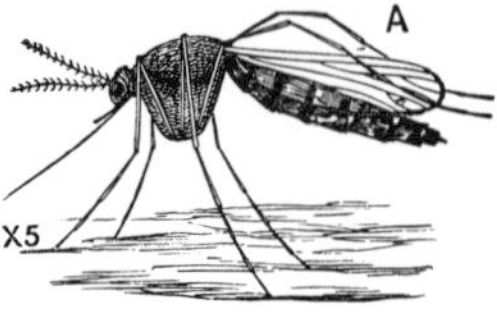

Mosquito 588R-MN

M

Meadow Lark 203R-MN
(*Sturnella magna*)

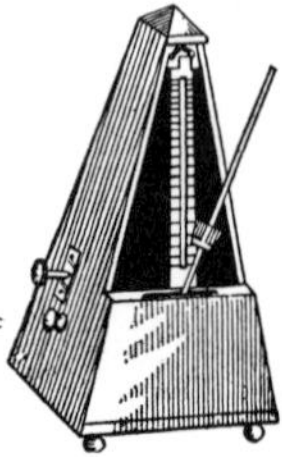

Metronome
525R-M

Mortar & Pestle
204R-M

Mermaid 239R-MN

Mammoth 401-W

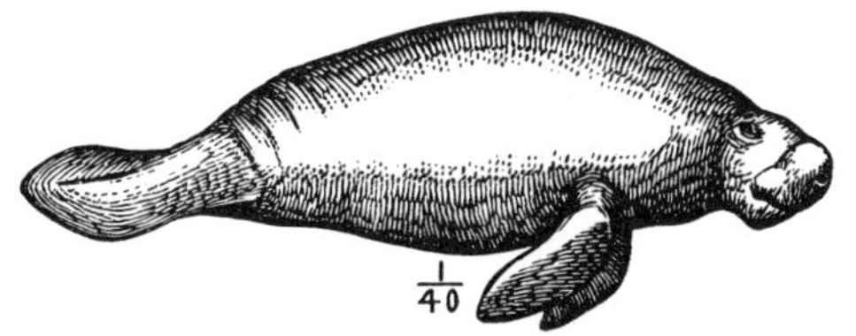

Manatee 574-WN
(*Trichechus americanus*)

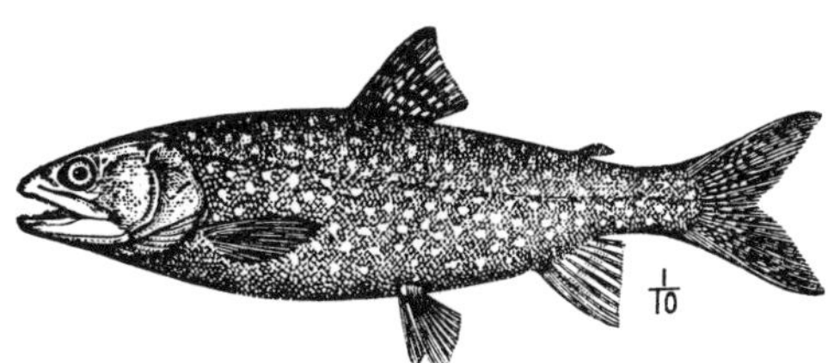

Malma (*Salvelinus malma*) 608R-W

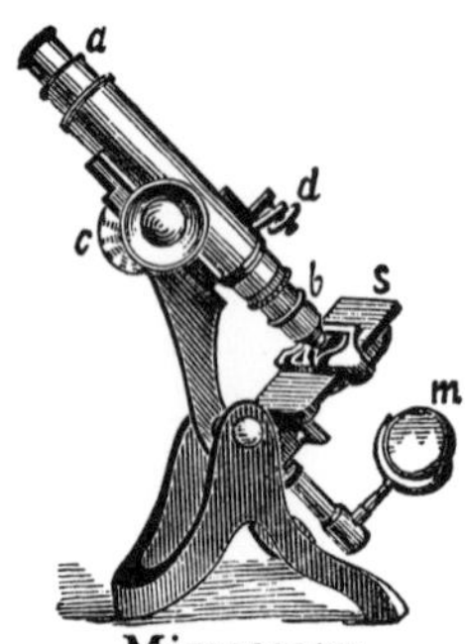

Microscope
320-MN

Melon Thistle Cactus
250R-W

Monkey
(*Cebidae*)
361R-W4

Monkey (c)
(*Lemuroidea*)
153-W4

Monkey (do)
(*Simiadae*)
154R-W4

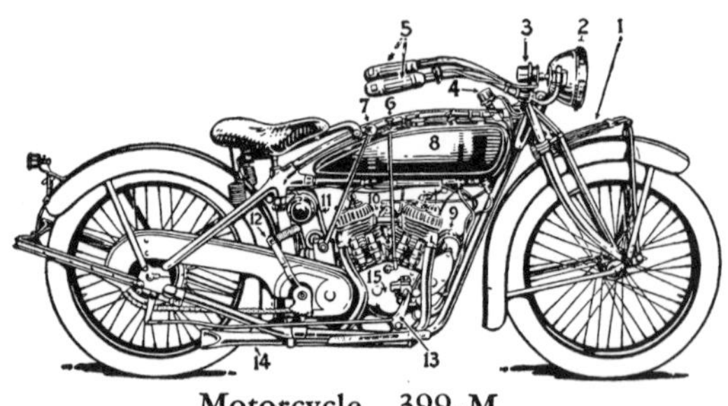

Motorcycle 399-M

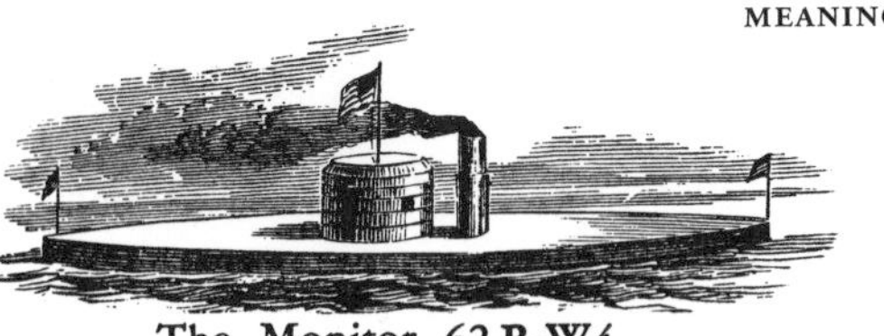

The Monitor 62 R-W4

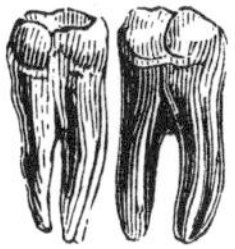

Molars
616 R-W4

1/3

Moloch
534-MN

M

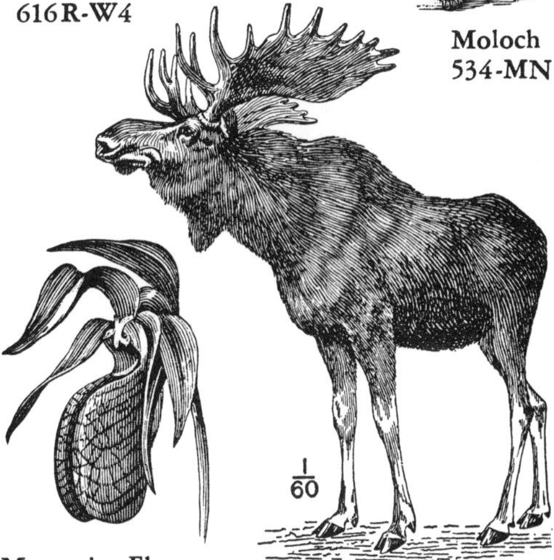

1/60

Moccasin Flower
(*Cypripedium acaule*)
563R-MN

Moose (*Alces machlis*)
251R-M

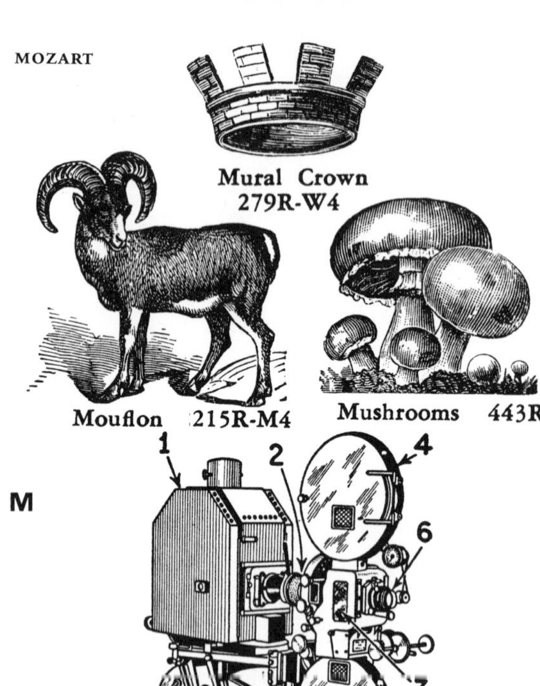

Mural Crown
279R-W4

Mouflon 215R-M4

Mushrooms 443R

M

1 2 3 4 5 6

Movie Projector K522-M

N

Narcissus
7089 R-MN

Neck Tie
1952 -M

Napiform
5272R-W4

Natant
6121R-WI

Nautilus
5904R-MN

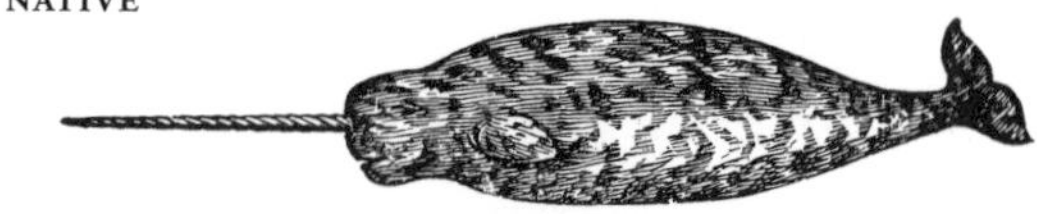

Narwhal (*Monodon monoceros*)
6405R-MN

Napu 6475R

Nepenthes
6523RN

N

Nimble Will
6333R-M

Night Heron
6254R-MN

Newel
6705R-MN

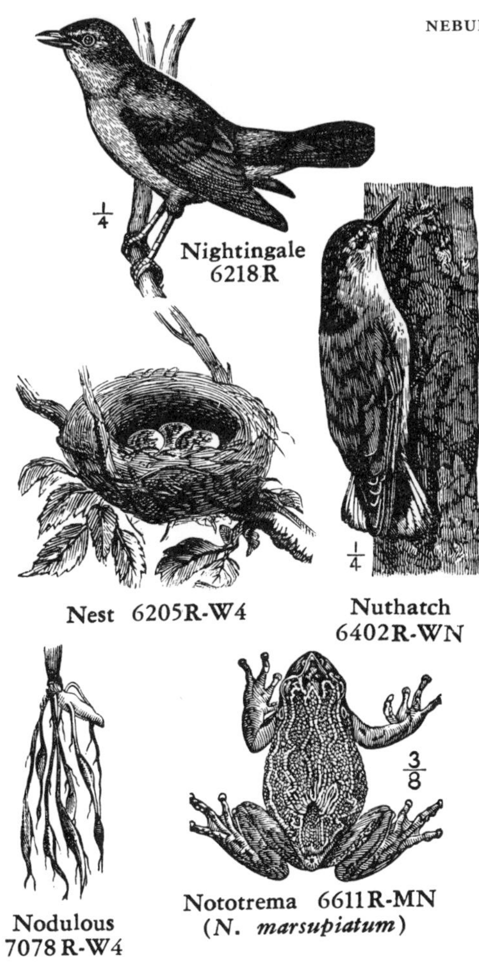

Nightingale
6218R

Nest 6205R-W4

Nuthatch
6402R-WN

Nodulous
7078R-W4

Nototrema 6611R-MN
(*N. marsupiatum*)

Neuroptera
6618 **R-WN**

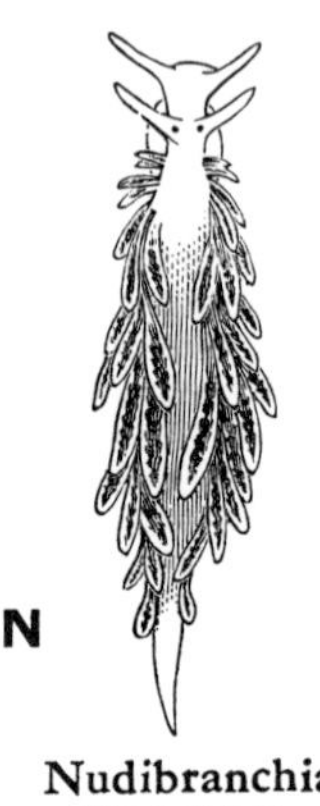

Nudibranchia
6514-**WN**

Nut
6273-**WN**

Nut Weevil
6531-**MN**
(*Balaninus nasicus*)

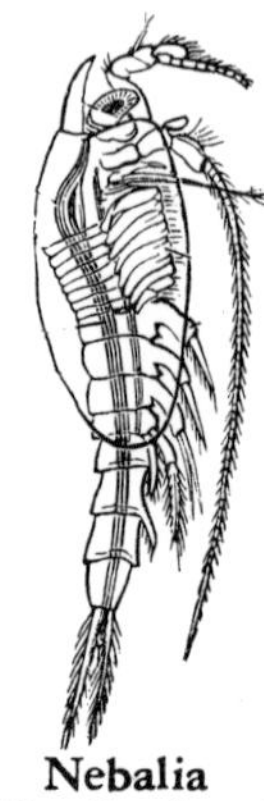

Nebalia
(*N. Geoffroyi*)
6613 **R-MN**

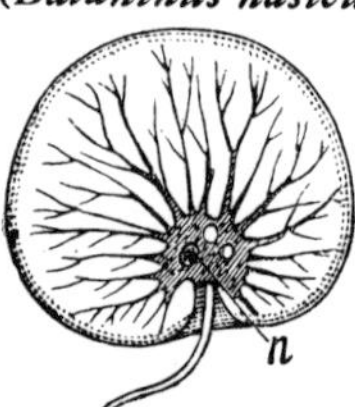

Noctiluca
6656 **R-MN**

O

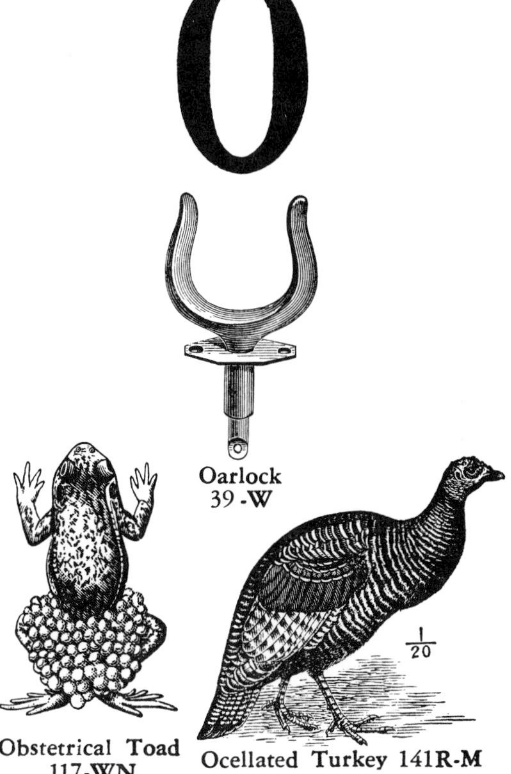

Oarlock
39-W

Obstetrical Toad
117-WN

Ocellated Turkey 141R-M

Ocelot 143-WN
(*Felis pardalis*)

Oboe (Hautboy) 153-WN

O

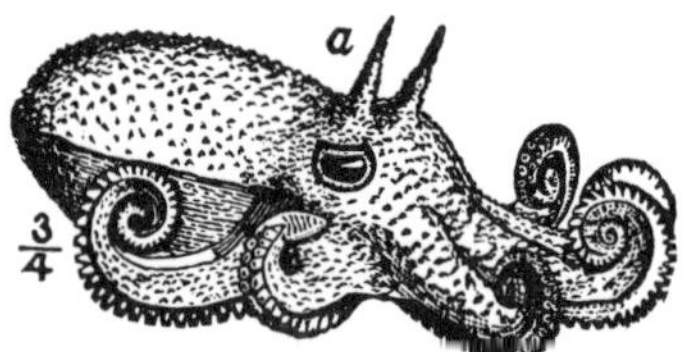

Octopus 169 R-MN

Ocypodian 213 R-W4

Onion Fly
219 R-MN

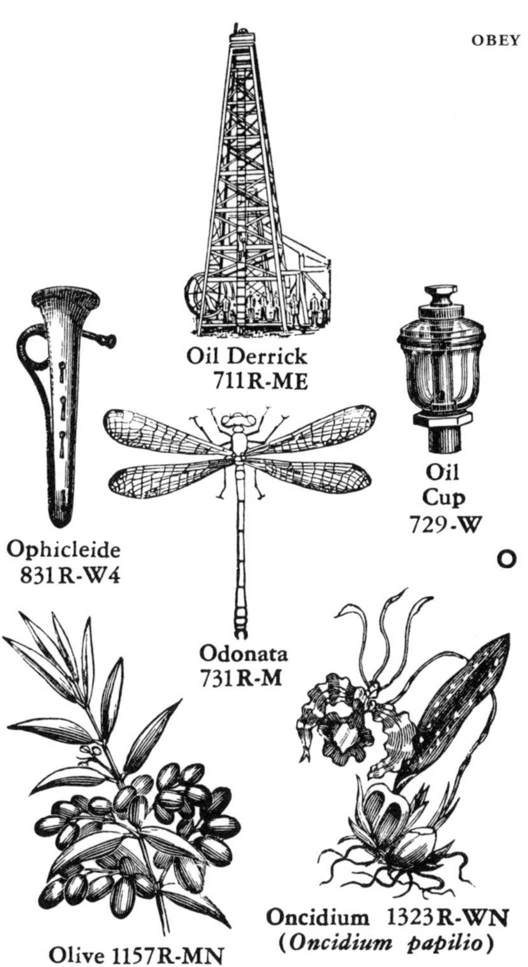

Oil Derrick 711R-ME

Oil Cup 729-W

Ophicleide 831R-W4

O

Odonata 731R-M

Olive 1157R-MN

Oncidium 1323R-WN (*Oncidium papilio*)

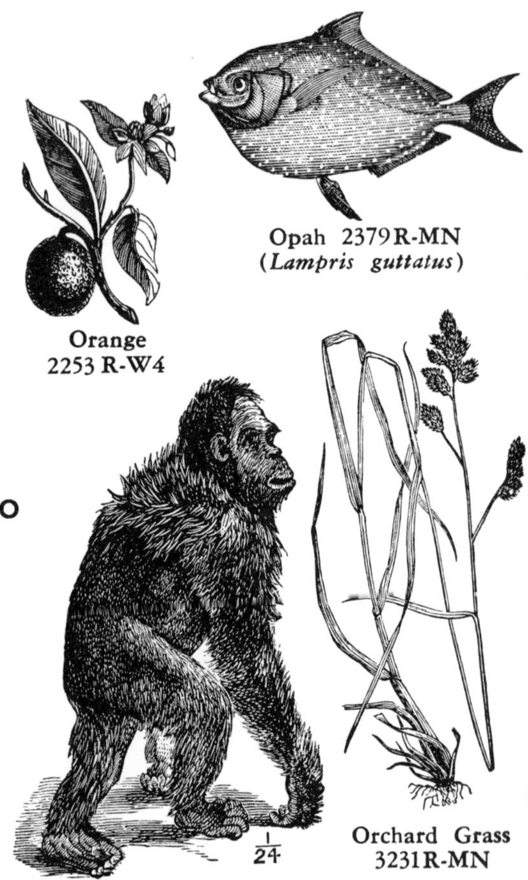

Opah 2379 R-MN
(*Lampris guttatus*)

Orange
2253 R-W4

Orchard Grass
3231 R-MN

Orangutan 3213-MN

Orchard Oriole & Nest
(*Icterus spurius*)
3379 -WN

Orchis
3531 R-W4

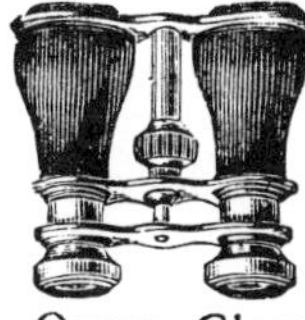

Opera Glass
3569R-MN

Orgyia
3771-WN O

Opossum 3795R-MN
(*Didelphis virginiana*)

Order Arms
4997R-MN

Orbiculate
5141R-W4

Ovate-
acuminate
5559-MN

Ovoid
5837R-M4

O

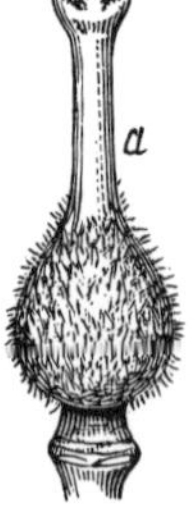

Ovary
(Plant)
6103-WN

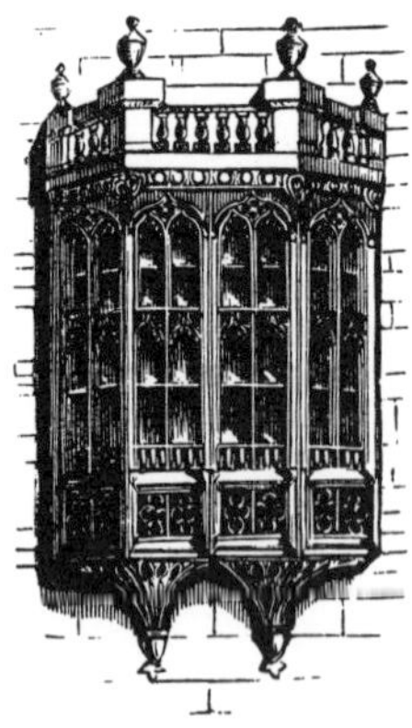

Oriel 6441R-W4

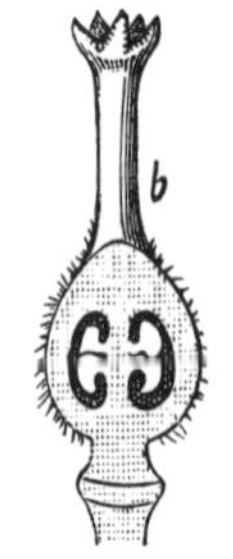

Ovary
(Plant)
6557-WN

Orrery 6561R-W4

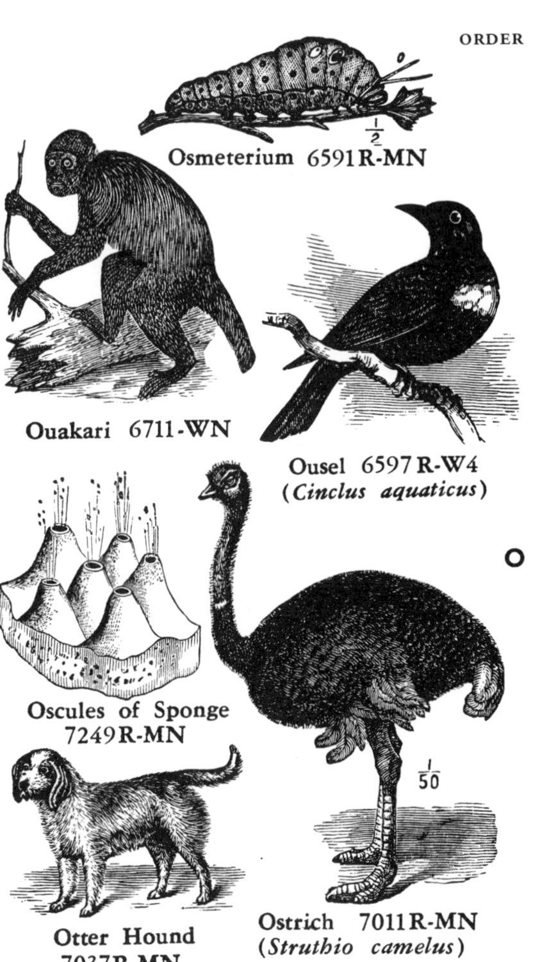

Osmeterium 6591 R-MN

Ouakari 6711-WN

Ousel 6597 R-W4
(*Cinclus aquaticus*)

O

Oscules of Sponge
7249 R-MN

Otter Hound
7037 R-MN

Ostrich 7011 R-MN
(*Struthio camelus*)

O Owlet 7353-WN (*Megascops flammeolus*)

Owl 7479-MN (Great Gray) (*Ulula cinerea*)

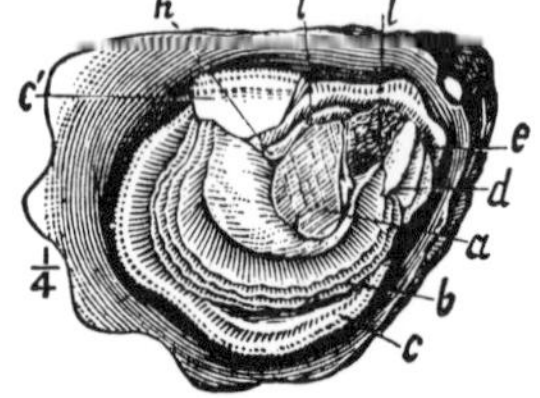

Oyster 7917-MN
a Muscle; b Gills; c'c Mantle; d Palpi; e Mouth; h Anus; *i* Intestine; l Liver

P

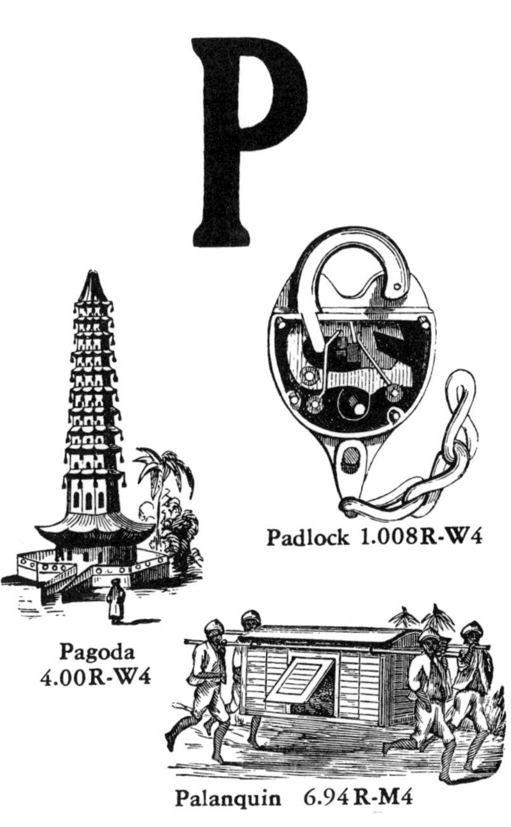

Padlock 1.008R-W4

Pagoda
4.00R-W4

Palanquin 6.94R-M4

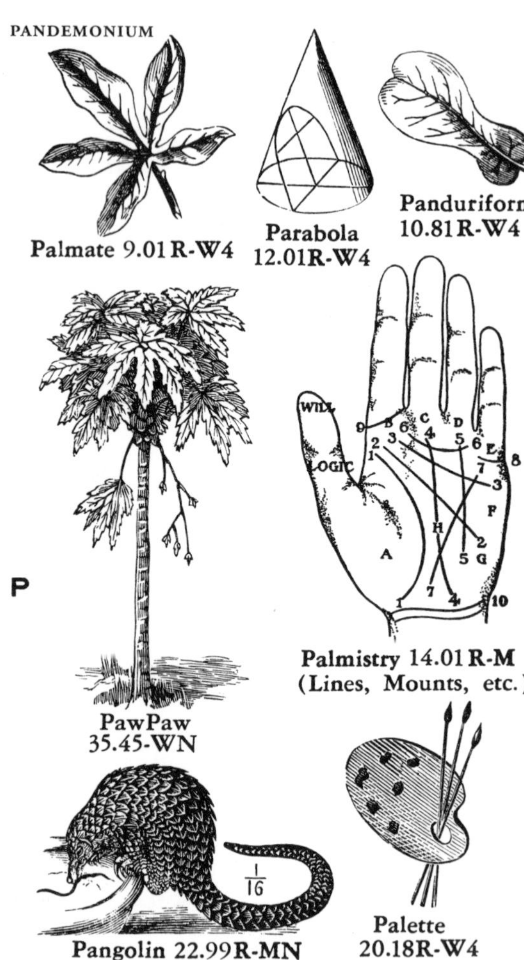

Palmate 9.01R-W4

Parabola 12.01R-W4

Panduriform 10.81R-W4

Palmistry 14.01R-M (Lines, Mounts, etc.)

PawPaw 35.45-WN

Pangolin 22.99R-MN

Palette 20.18R-W4

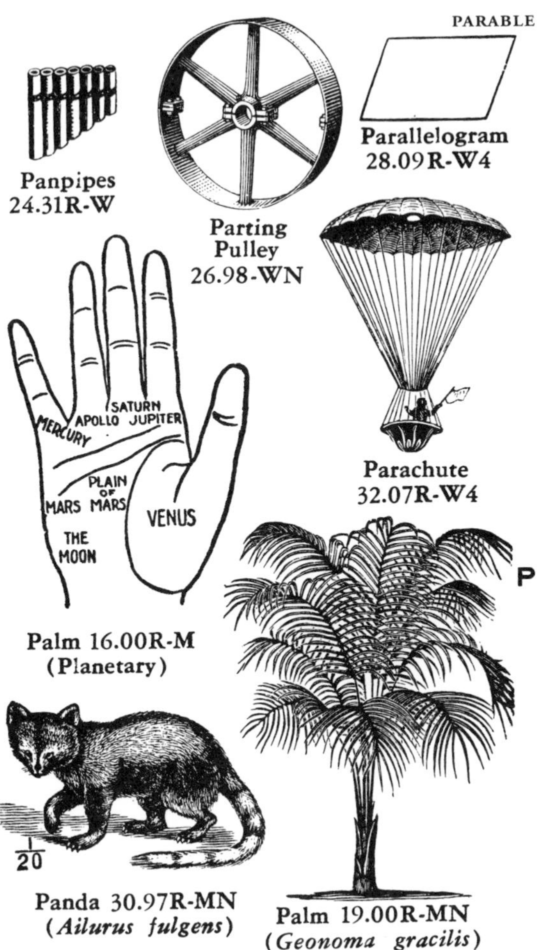

Panpipes
24.31R-W

Parting
Pulley
26.98-WN

Parallelogram
28.09R-W4

Parachute
32.07R-W4

Palm 16.00R-M
(Planetary)

Panda 30.97R-MN
(*Ailurus fulgens*)

Palm 19.00R-MN
(*Geonoma gracilis*)

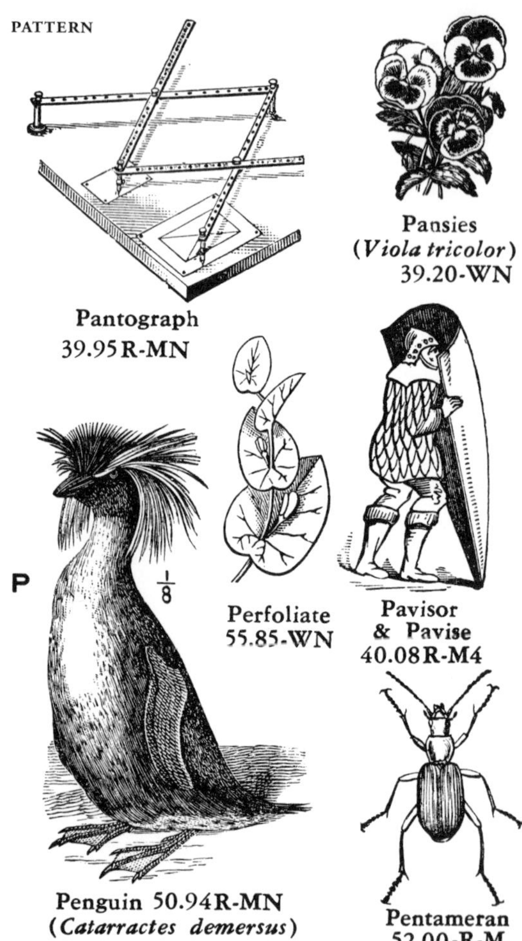

Pantograph
39.95R-MN

Pansies
(*Viola tricolor*)
39.20-WN

Perfoliate
55.85-WN

Pavisor
& Pavise
40.08R-M4

Penguin 50.94R-MN
(*Catarractes demersus*)

Pentameran
52.00-R-M

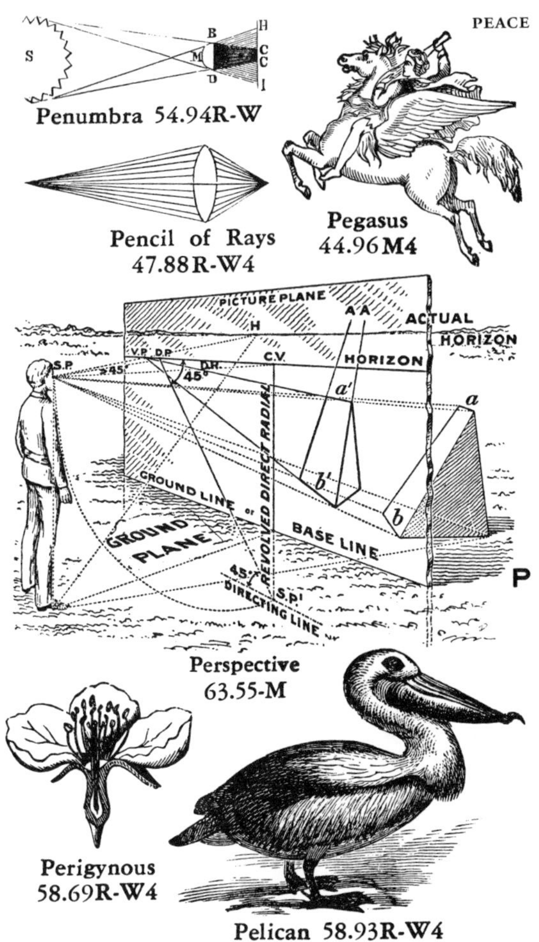

Penumbra 54.94R-W

Pencil of Rays 47.88R-W4

Pegasus 44.96M4

Perspective 63.55-M

Perigynous 58.69R-W4

Pelican 58.93R-W4

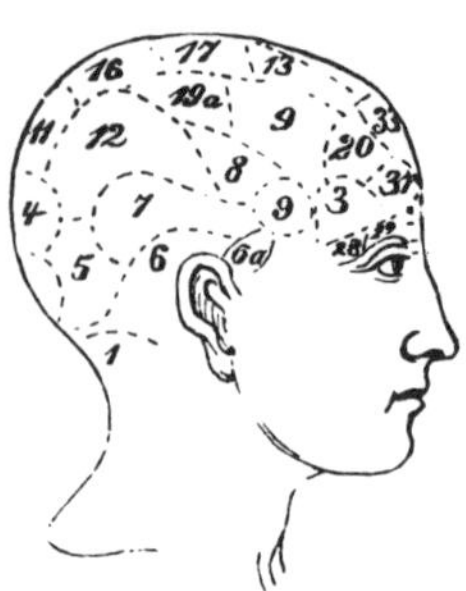

Phrenology
65.39R-M4

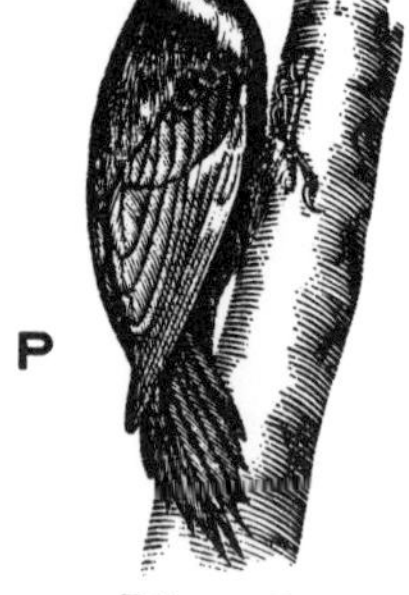

P

Pileated
Woodpecker
69.72-**WN**

Pillory 72.61**R-W4**

Pillow Block
74.92-**WN**

Pipe 79.90-M

Paris
78.96-ML

Portrait
of the Artist
1076R-W4

Pinnacle
83.80R-W4

Pipa (*P. americana*) 85.47R-MN

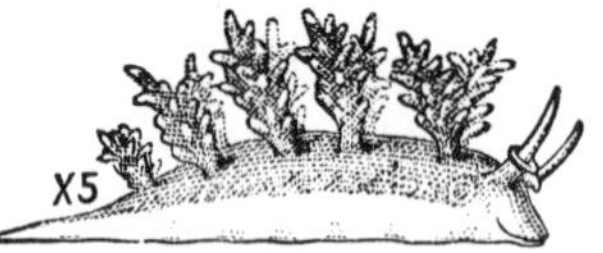

Polybranchia 102.9R-MN

Pleurotoma (*P. babylonica*)
95.94**R-WN**

Pliers
(98)**R-W4**

Plane 88.91**R-M**

P

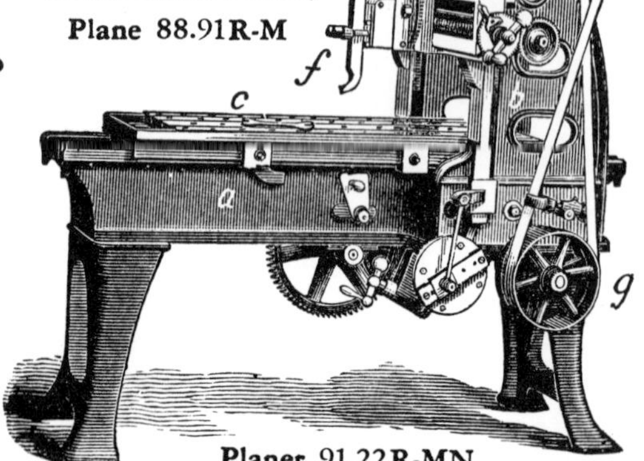

Planer 91.22**R-MN**
a Bed; b Upright; c Table; d Crosshead

Plantain Tree 92.91R-W4
(*Musa paradisiaca*)

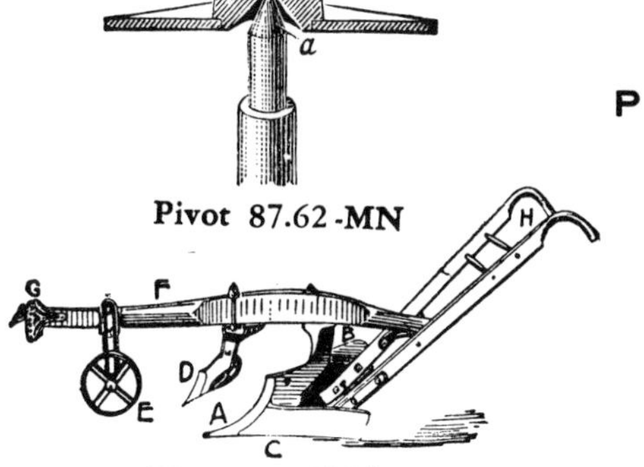

Pivot 87.62-MN

Plow 101.0R-M
A Share; B Moldboard; C Landside;
D Jointer; E Gauge wheel; F Beam;
G Clevis; H Handles

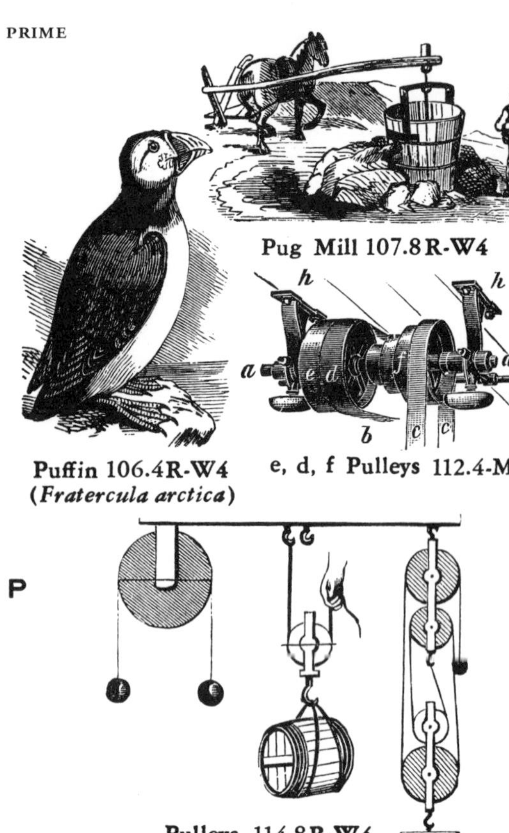

Pug Mill 107.8R-W4

Puffin 106.4R-W4
(*Fratercula arctica*)

e, d, f Pulleys 112.4-MN

P

Pulleys 114.8R-W4
(Single fixed, Fall & Tackle)

Q

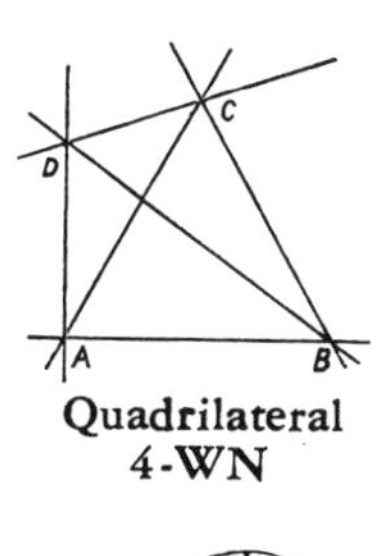

Quadrilateral
4-WN

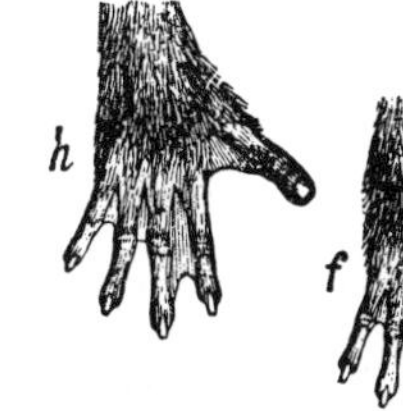

Quadrumana
10 R-MN

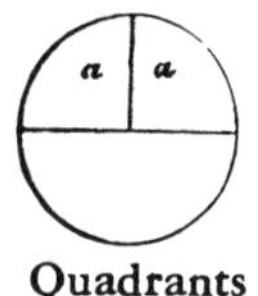

Quadrants
11-WN

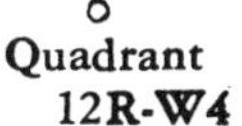

Quadrant
12R-W4

Quail 13 R-MN
(*Callipepla californica*)

Quail 14 R-MN
(*Coturnix communis*)
a Adult; b Young

Q

Quagga (*Equus quagga*)
20 R-MN

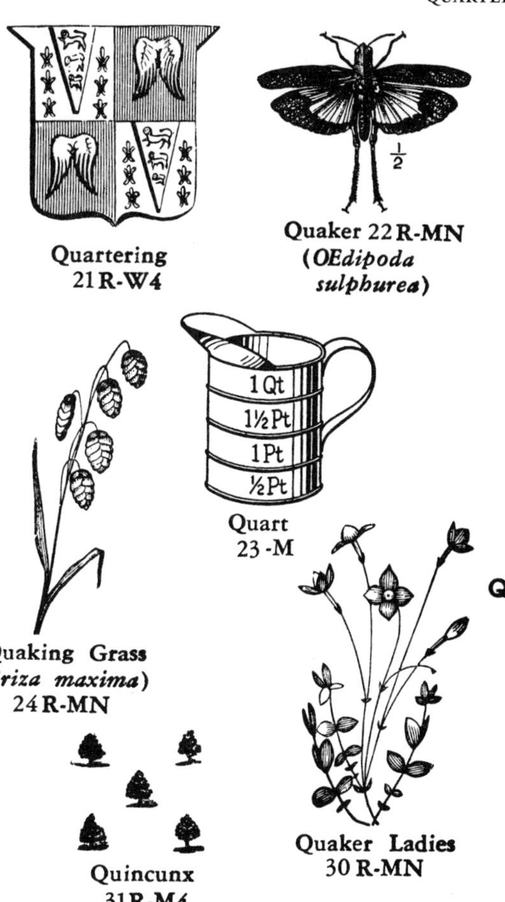

Quartering
21 R-W4

Quaker 22 R-MN
(*OEdipoda sulphurea*)

Quart
23 -M

Quaking Grass
(*Briza maxima*)
24 R-MN

Quincunx
31 R-M4

Quaker Ladies
30 R-MN

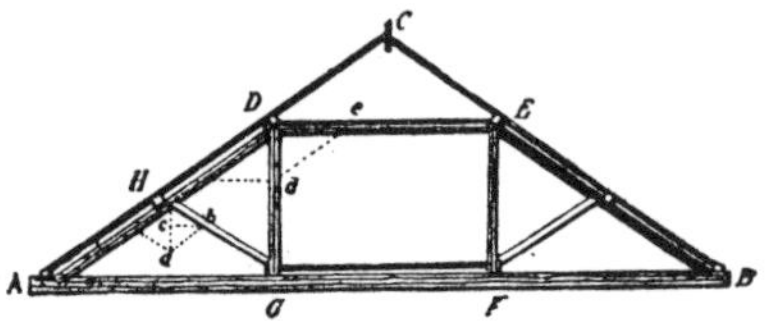

Queen-Post Roof 32R-MN

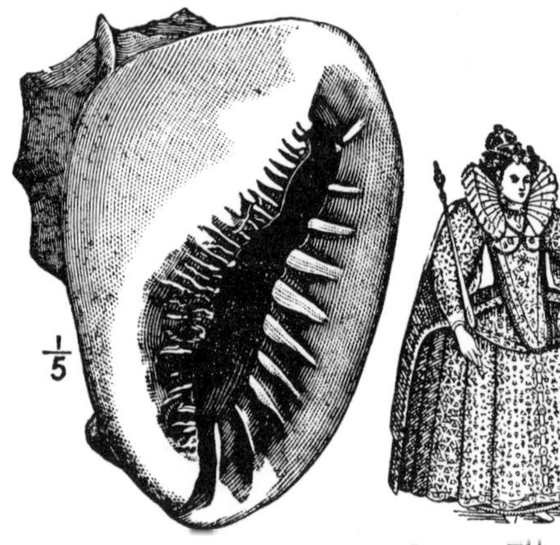

Queen Conch 33R-MN
(*Cassis cameo*)

Queen Elizabeth
34R-ML

Quinnat 40R-MN

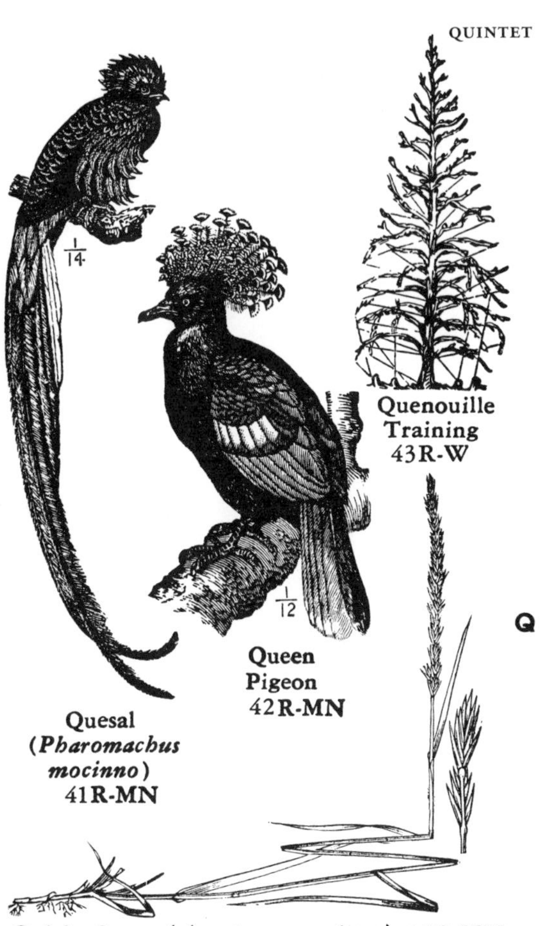

Quenouille Training 43R-W

Queen Pigeon 42R-MN

Quesal (*Pharomachus mocinno*) 41R-MN

Quick Grass (*Agropyrum repens*) 44R-MN

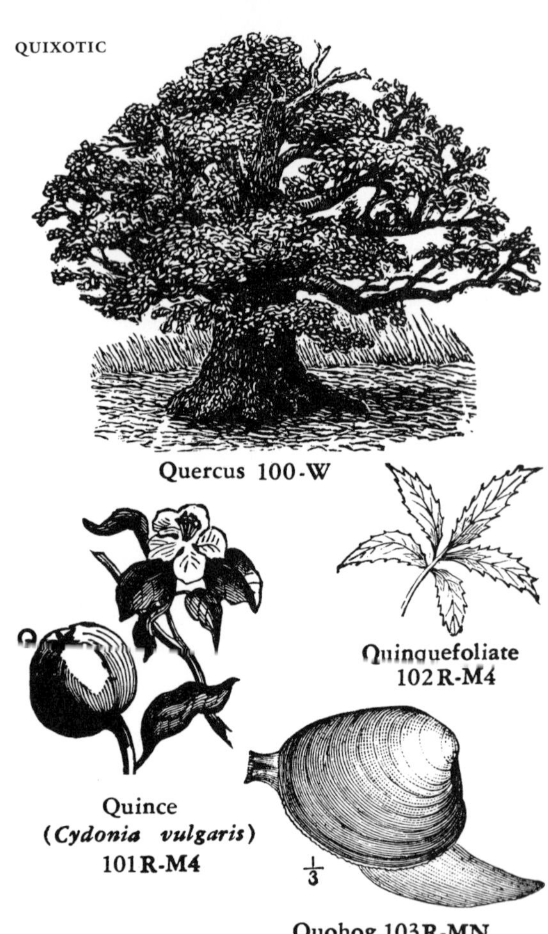

Quercus 100-W

Quinquefoliate
102 R-M4

Quince
(*Cydonia vulgaris*)
101 R-M4

Quohog 103 R-MN
(*Venus mercenaria*)

R

Raceme
2213-W4

Rabbit 2297-WN

Radius
2075R-W4

Raccoon 1996-WN

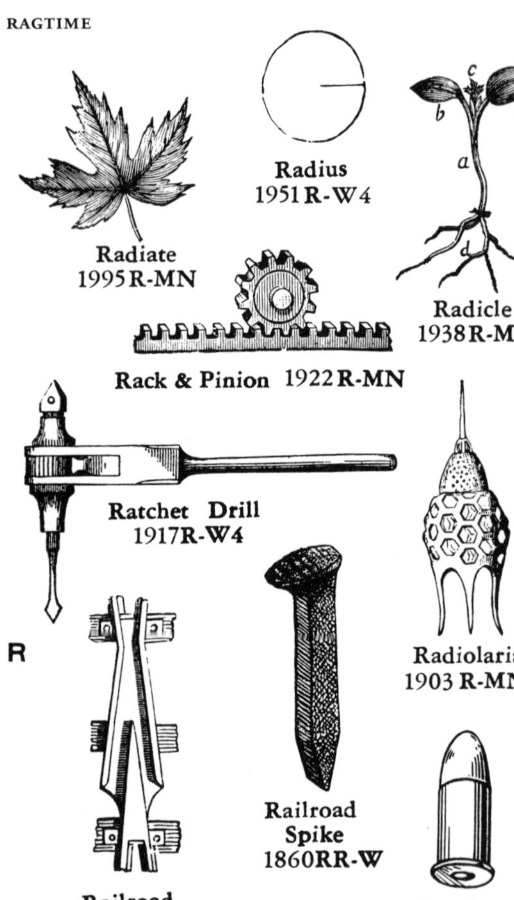

Radiate
1995 R-MN

Radius
1951 R-W4

Radicle
1938 R-MN

Rack & Pinion 1922 R-MN

Ratchet Drill
1917R-W4

Radiolaria
1903 R-MN

Railroad
Spike
1860RR-W

Railroad
Frog
1893 R-W4

Revolver
Cartridge
1844 -M

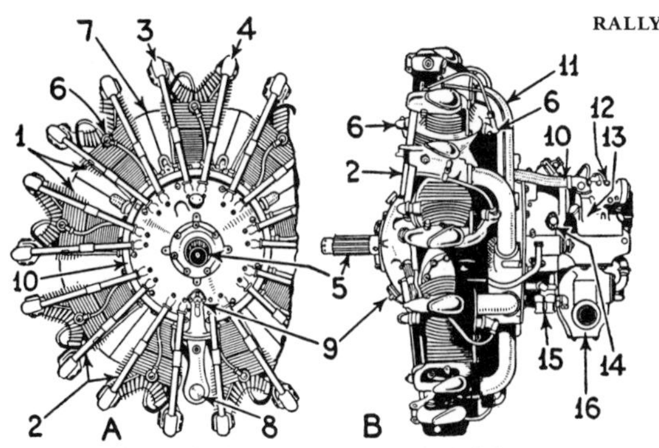

Radial Airplane Engine 1839-M

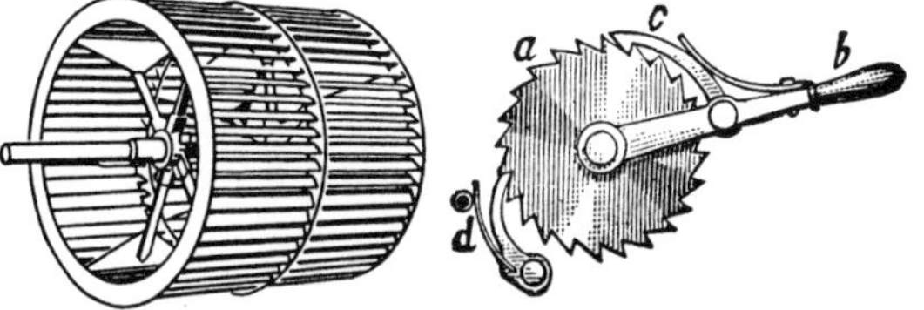

Rat Race 1836-M

Ratchet Wheel 1835-M

R

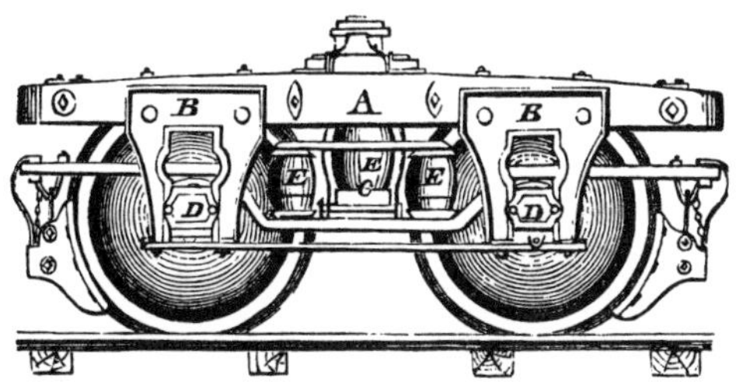

Railway Truck 1833R-W4

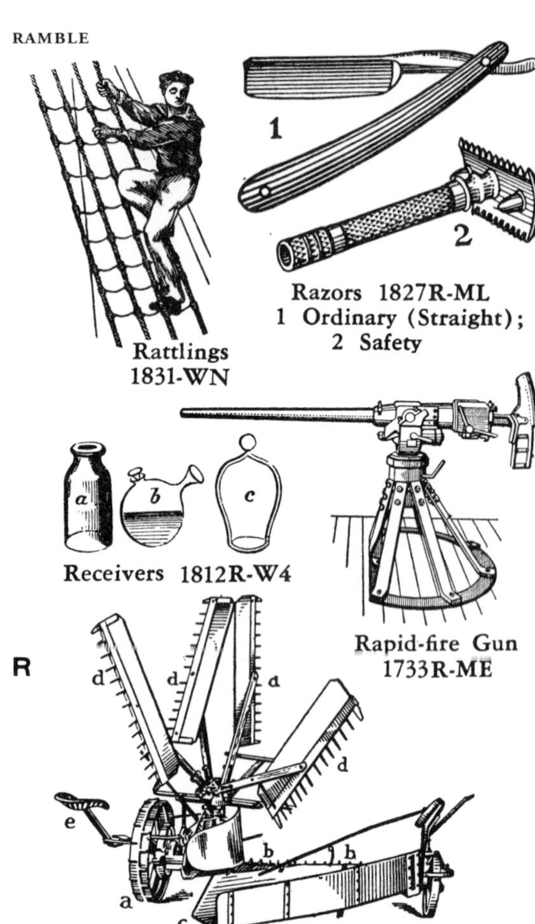

Rattlings 1831-WN

Razors 1827R-ML
1 Ordinary (Straight);
2 Safety

Receivers 1812R-W4

Rapid-fire Gun 1733R-ME

R

Reaper 1704R-ME

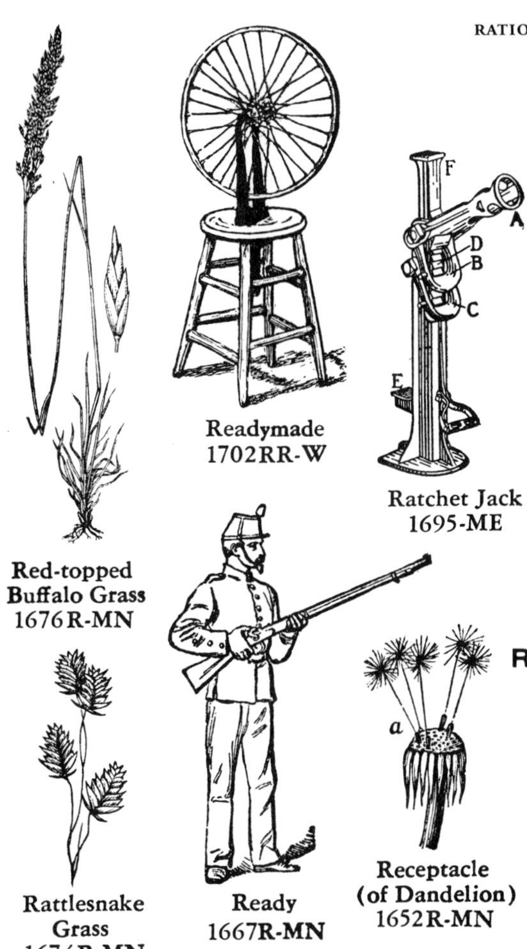

Readymade
1702RR-W

Ratchet Jack
1695-ME

Red-topped
Buffalo Grass
1676R-MN

Rattlesnake
Grass
1674R-MN

Ready
1667R-MN

Receptacle
(of Dandelion)
1652R-MN

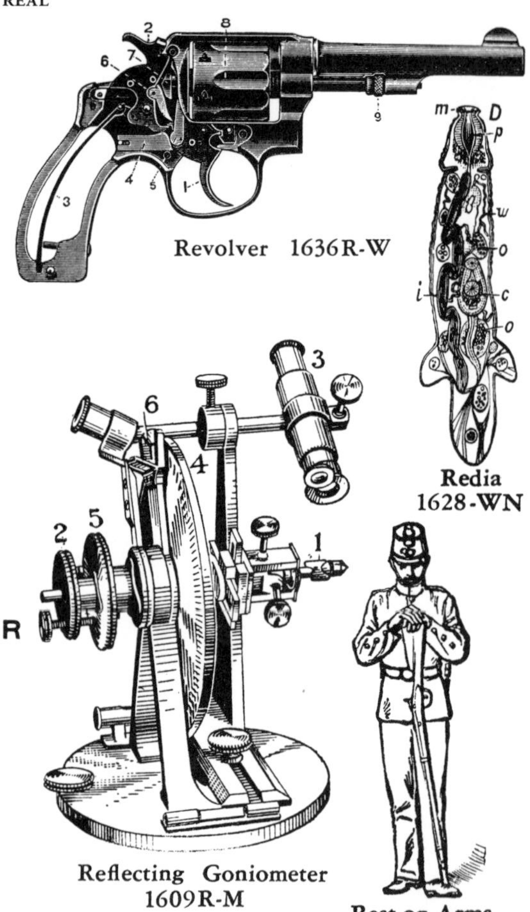

Revolver 1636R-W

Redia
1628-WN

Reflecting Goniometer
1609R-M

Rest on Arms
1599R MN

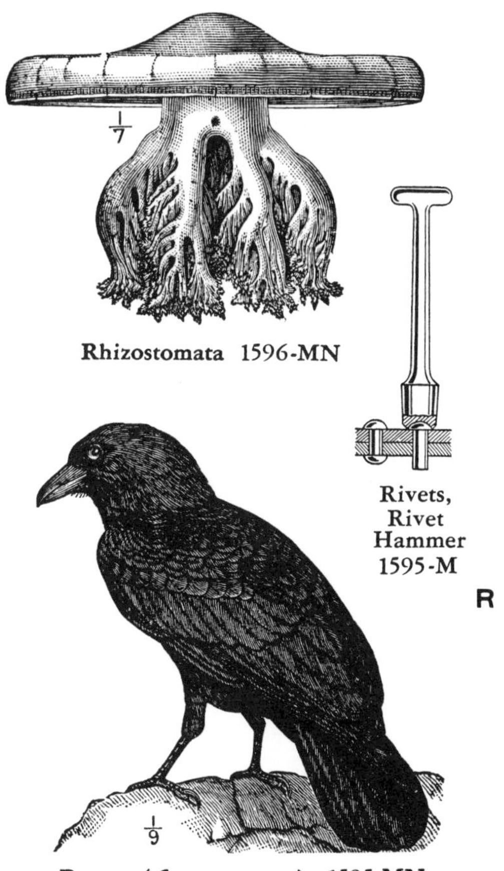

Rhizostomata 1596-MN

Rivets, Rivet Hammer 1595-M

Raven (*Corvus corax*) 1595-MN

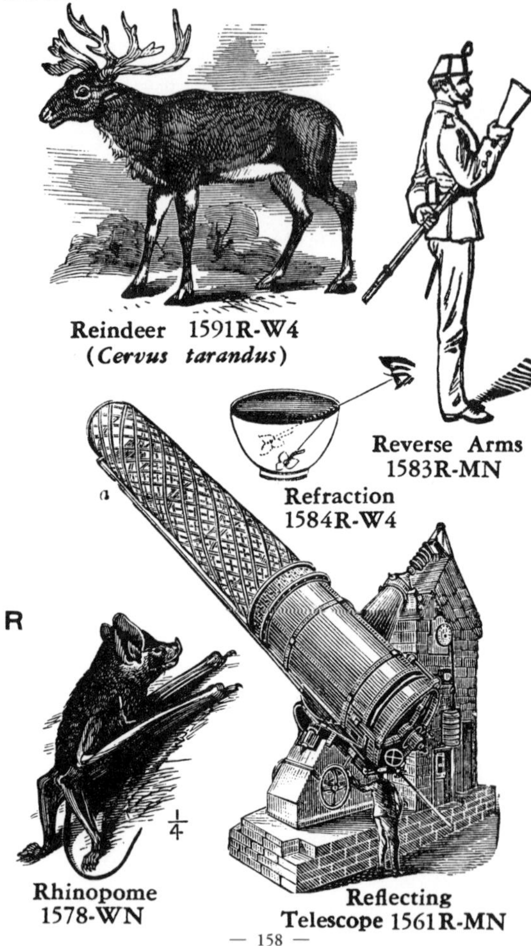

Reindeer 1591R-W4
(*Cervus tarandus*)

Reverse Arms
1583R-MN

Refraction
1584R-W4

Rhinopome
1578-WN

Reflecting
Telescope 1561R-MN

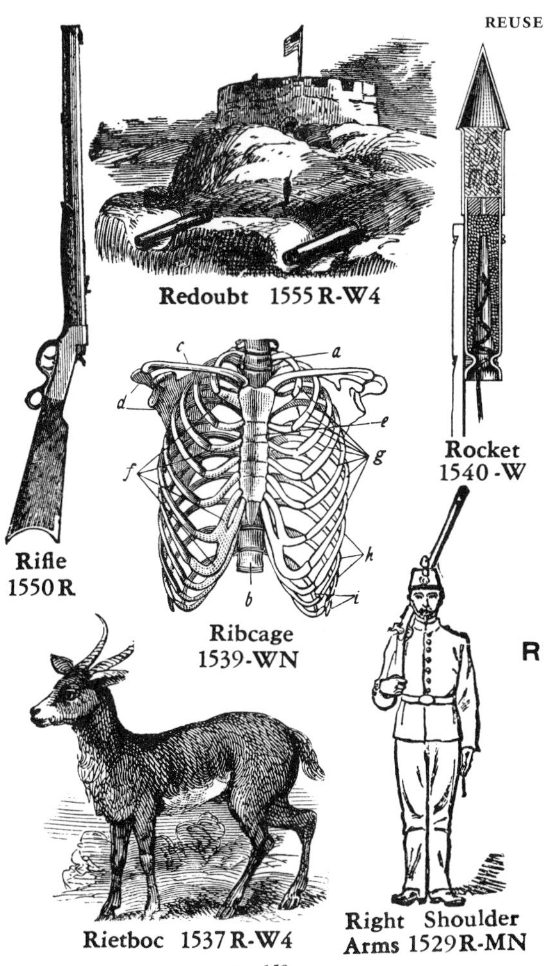

Redoubt 1555 R-W4

Rocket
1540 -W

Rifle
1550 R

Ribcage
1539-WN

R

Rietboc 1537 R-W4

Right Shoulder
Arms 1529 R-MN

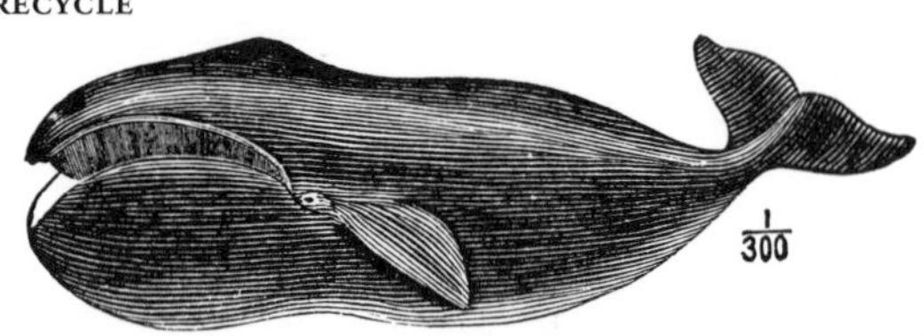

Right Whale (*Balaena mysticetus*)
1529-**M**

Rubythroated
Hummingbird
1525-**MN**

Rooster 1518R-M

R

Roller Skate
1512 -**M**

Root 1509-**W**

S

Sails 1789-M4

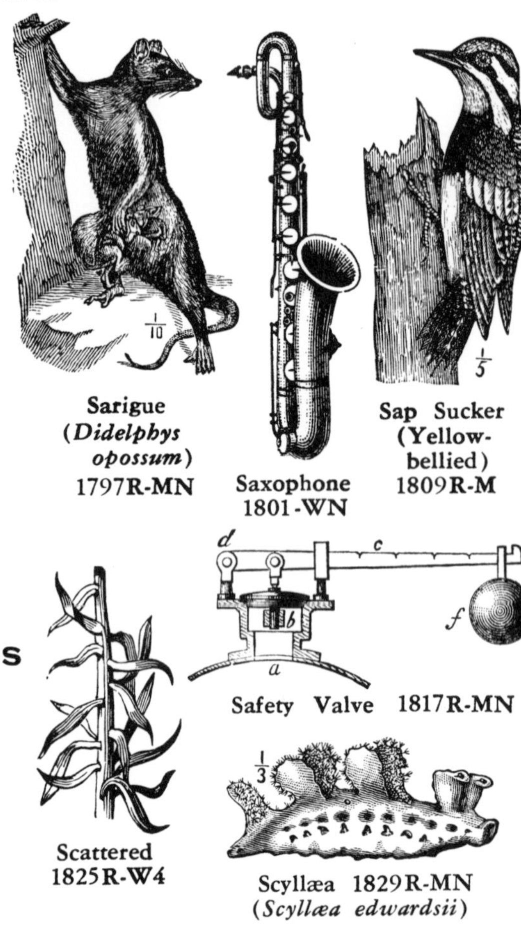

Sarigue (*Didelphys opossum*) 1797**R-MN**

Saxophone 1801-**WN**

Sap Sucker (Yellow-bellied) 1809**R-M**

S

Safety Valve 1817**R-MN**

Scattered 1825**R-W4**

Scyllæa 1829**R-MN** (*Scyllæa edwardsii*)

Scepter
1837R-W4

Screw
1841-WN
a Male
b Female

Sequoia
1845-WN

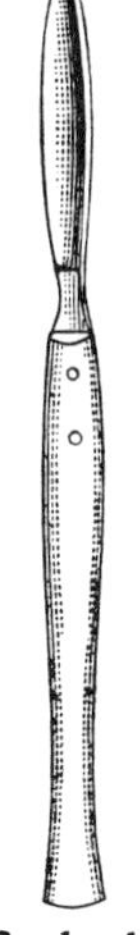

Scalpel
1841-WN

S

Scorpioid
1849R-WN

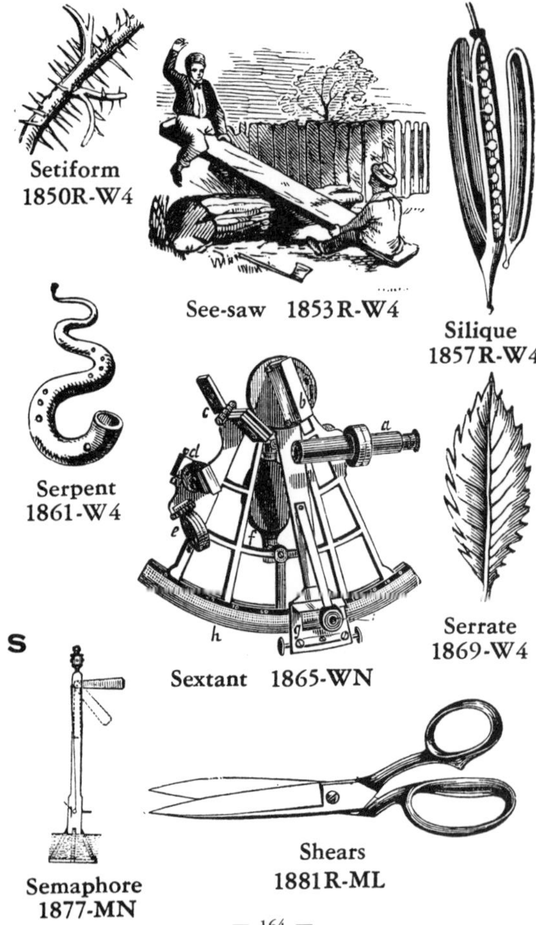

Setiform
1850R-W4

See-saw 1853R-W4

Silique
1857R-W4

Serpent
1861-W4

Sextant 1865-WN

Serrate
1869-W4

S

Semaphore
1877-MN

Shears
1881R-ML

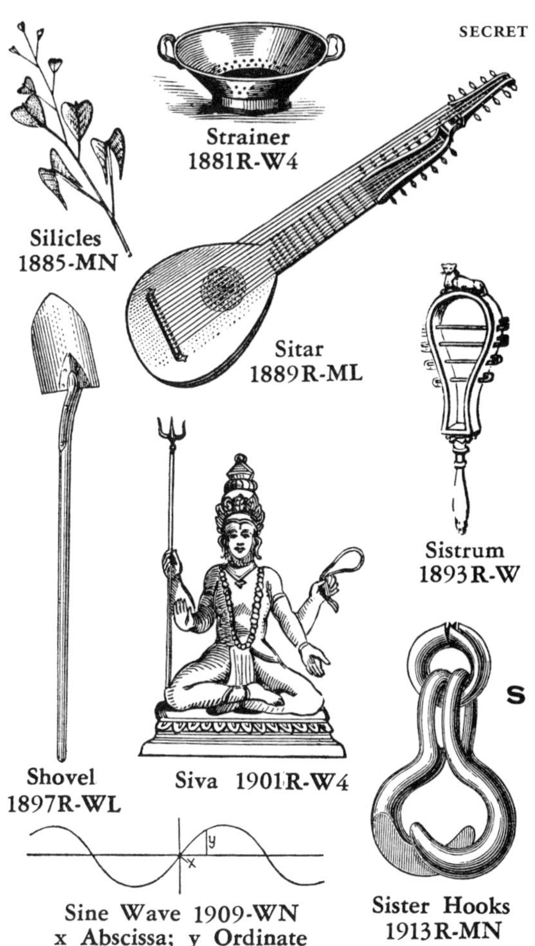

Strainer
1881R-W4

Silicles
1885-MN

Sitar
1889R-ML

Sistrum
1893R-W

Shovel
1897R-WL

Siva 1901R-W4

Sine Wave 1909-WN
x Abscissa; y Ordinate

Sister Hooks
1913R-MN

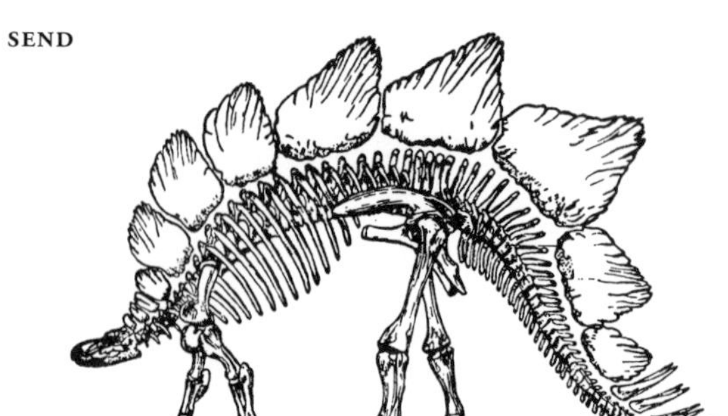

Skeleton of Stegosaurus 1921 R-M

Slinging Barrels
1923 R-ML

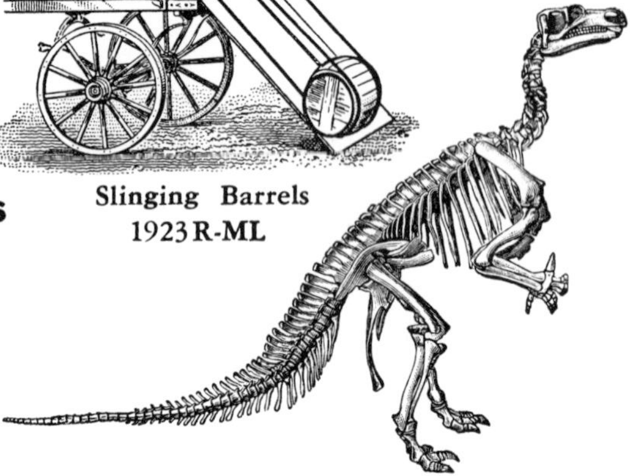

Skeleton of Iguanodon 1929 R-MN

Skeleton of Ichthyosaurus 1933R-W4

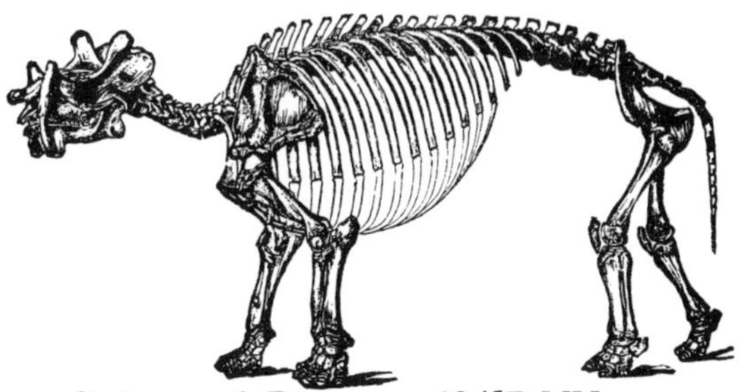

Skeleton of Dinoceras 1945R-MN

Spiralozooids
1953-WN

Spinning Wheel
1961-WN

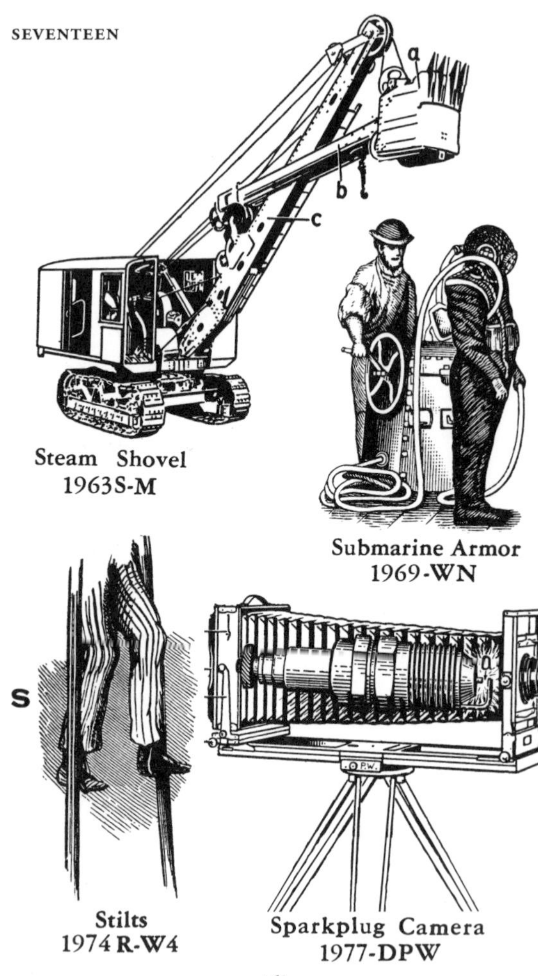

SEVENTEEN

Steam Shovel
1963S-M

Submarine Armor
1969-WN

Stilts
1974R-W4

Sparkplug Camera
1977-DPW

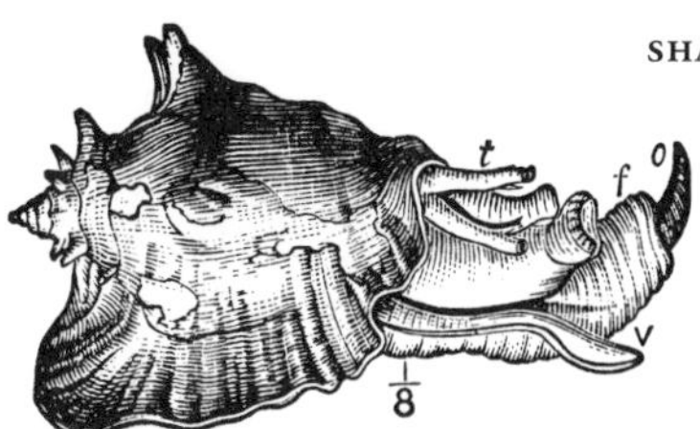

Strombus (*S. gigas*) 1981-MN

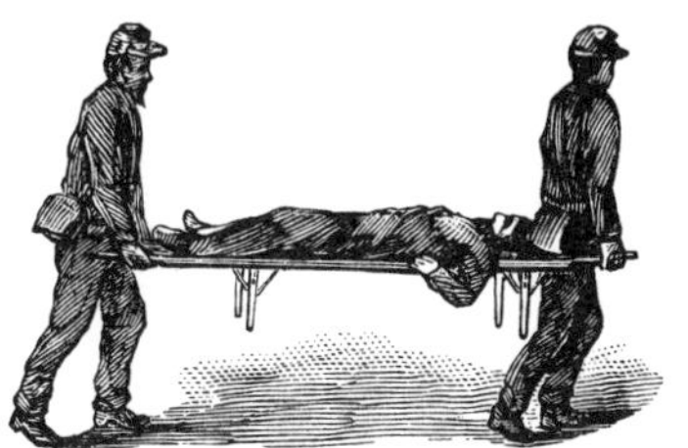

Stretcher 1989-WN

Still 1993R-WN
a Boiler; b Head; c Tube; s Worm; d Receiver

S

Swan Dive 2001-M

S

Surrender
2009-M

T

Table Saw 428-WN

Tam-tam
378R-W4

Tambourine 292-W

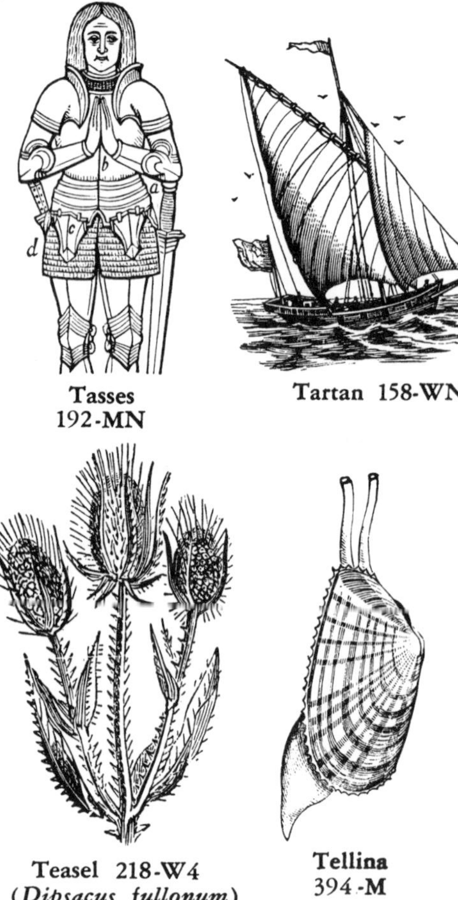

Tasses
192-MN

Tartan 158-WN

T

Teasel 218-W4
(*Dipsacus fullonum*)

Tellina
394-M

Telephone 428-M

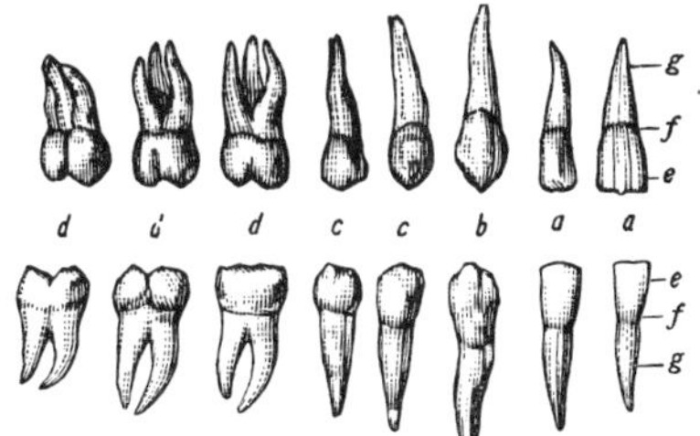

Teeth of Man 274-W
aa Incisors; b Canines; cc Bicuspids; ddd Molars; e Crown; f Neck; g Root

Tendrac 496 R-MN
(*Ericulus spinosus*)

Terrier (English)
160-MN

Terminus
180R-W4

Terebra
557-WN

Toga 756-WN
(Caius Marius)

Toggle Joint
268R-M4

T

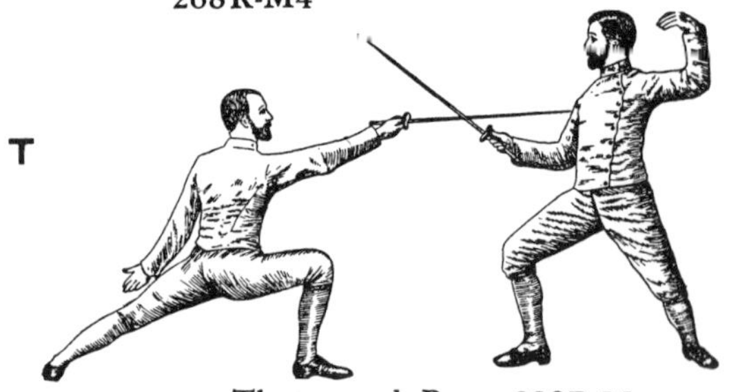

Thrust and Parry 220R-M
"Elzavir!"

Thoth
396R-W4

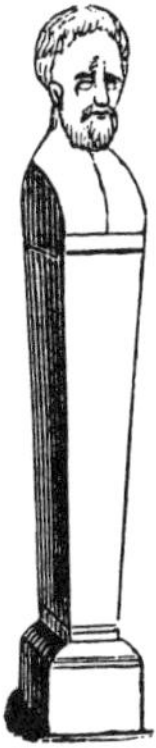

Terminus
440R-W4

Toga 434R-W4

Tower 476R-W4
Is it real?

Toad 553-MN
(*Bufo lentiginosus*)

½

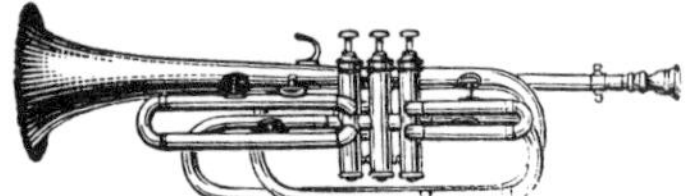

Trumpet 751-WN

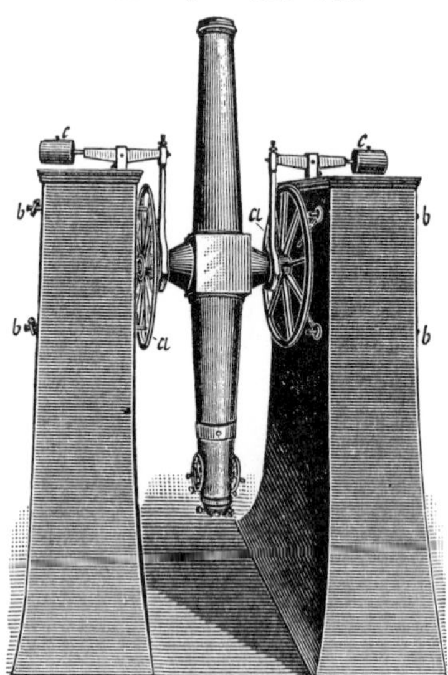

T

Transit Instrument 750-WN

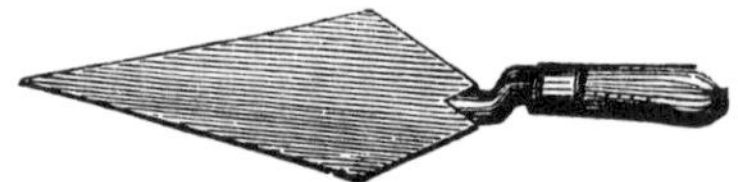

Trowel 758R-M4

Treadmill 666R-W4

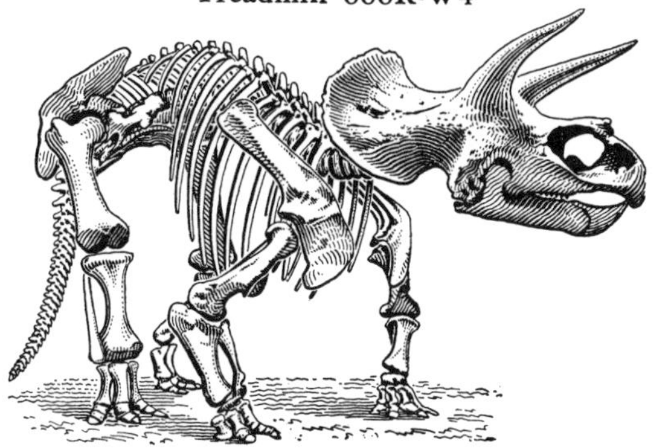

Triceratops 452-M

Troilus
492R-MN

Turnstile
504-W

Tulip Poplar
(*Liriodendron tulipifera*)
550-WN

1/8

Type
584R-W4
a Body;
b Face;
c Shoulder;
d Nick;
e Groove

Top
318-W

T

Tuba
550R-M

Umbonate
.01 R-W4

Umbrella Shell
.05 R-M

Umbrella Ant
.10 -MN

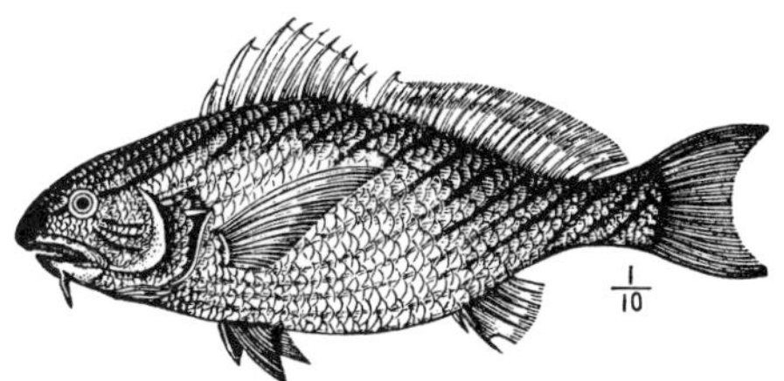

Umbra (*Umbrina cirrhosa*) .25-MN

Una Boat .50-WN

Unau 1R-MN
(*Cholopus didactylus*)

Unfix Bayonet
2R-MN

U

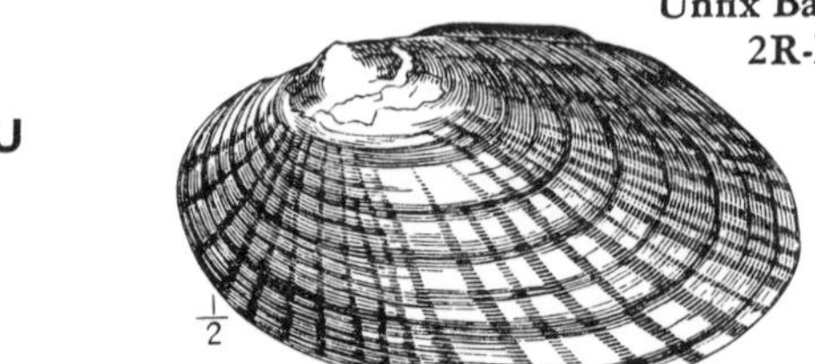

Unio (*U. radiatus*) 5-W

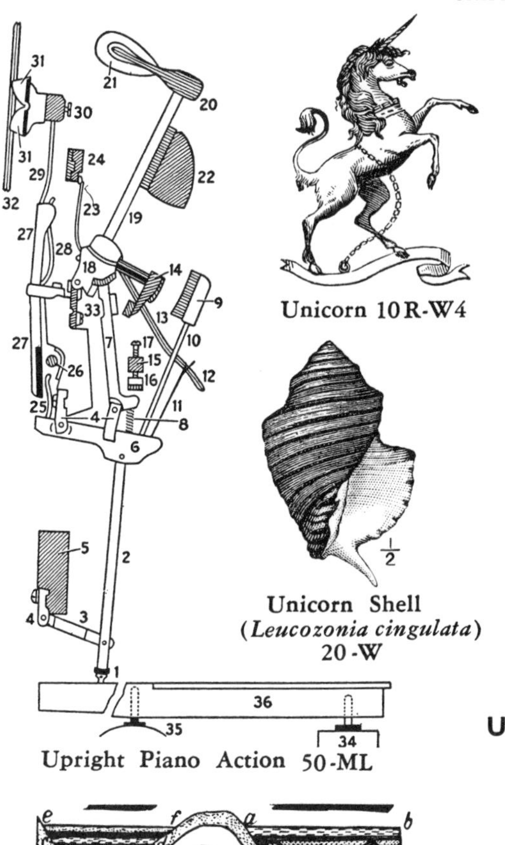

Unicorn 10R-W4

Unicorn Shell
(*Leucozonia cingulata*)
20-W

Upright Piano Action 50-ML

U

Unconformability 100-WN

Urodela (*Desmognathus fuscus*)
500-WN

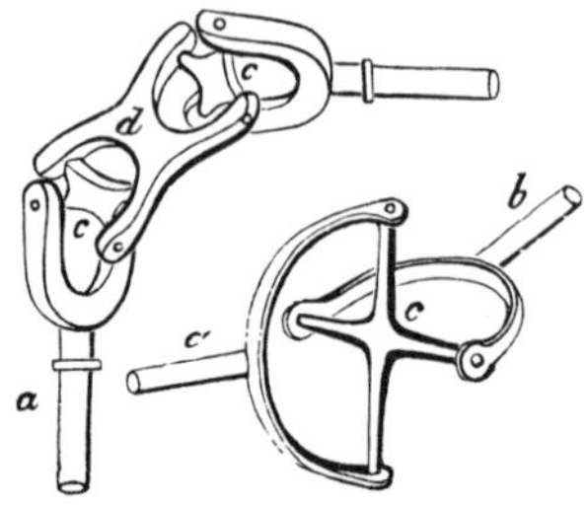

Universal Joints 1000R-W4

U

Ursula 10000-MN
(*Limenitis astyanax*)

V

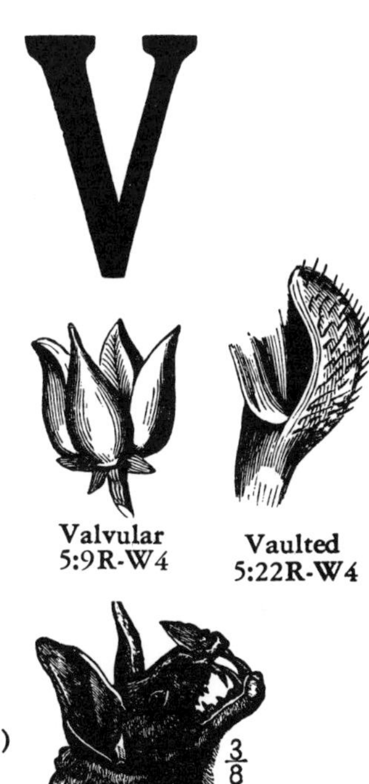

Vaginicola
(*V. cristalina*)
5:6 -WN

Valvular
5:9R-W4

Vaulted
5:22R-W4

3/8

Vampire 5:39-MN
(*Vampyrus spectrum*)
(False Vampire)

Varuna 5:44R-W4

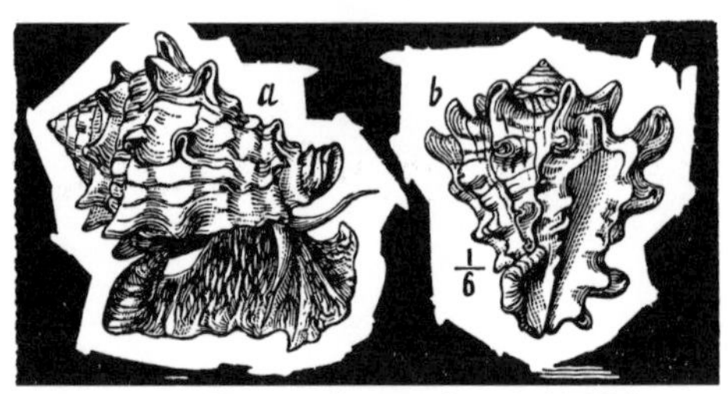

Vasum (*V. cornigerum*) 6:6-WN
a Side view with Animal; b Front of Shell

V

Velocipede 6:9-M

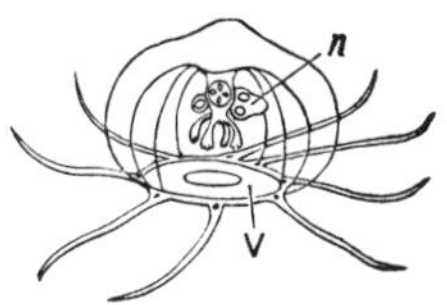

Velum 6:10R-MN
(of *Dysmorphosa fulgurans*)
n Young Zooids budding

Venus Flytrap
(*Dionæa muscipula*)
6:11R-W4

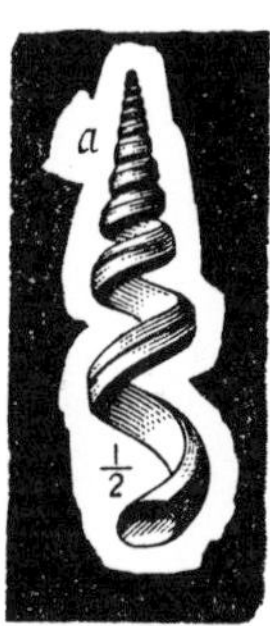

Vermetus
6:12-W

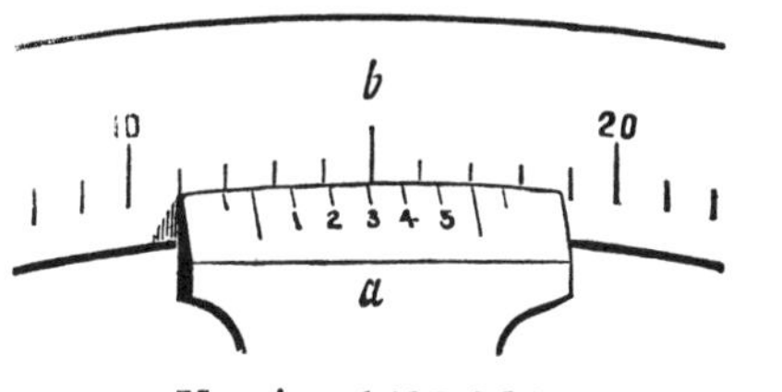

Vernier 6:13R-M4

Victorine
6:14R-W4

Grivet
(Not Vervet)
6:15R-WN

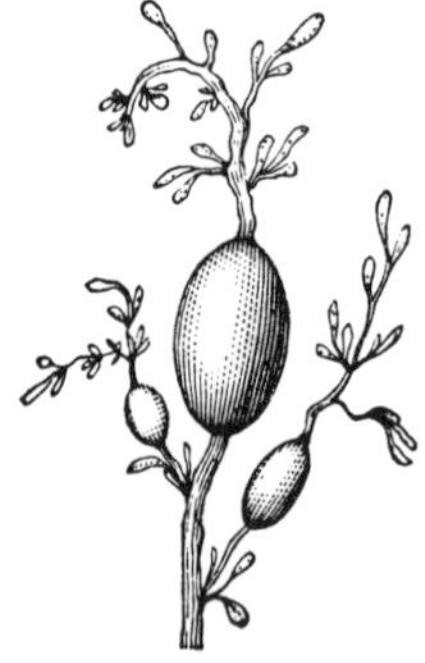

Vesicles
6:19R-MN
(*Fucus nodosus*)

Veranda 6:21R-W4

V

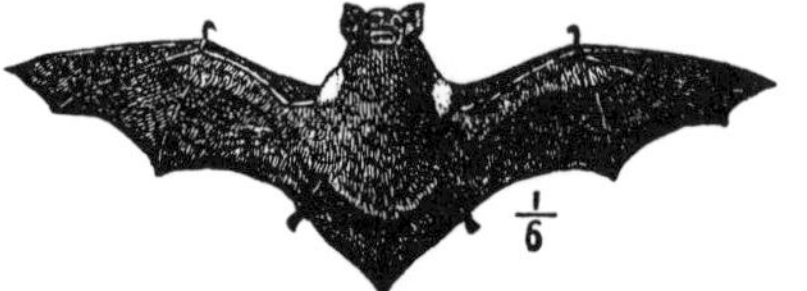

Vespertiliones 6:25-MN
(American Red Bat)

Viceroy Butterfly 6:27R-MN
(*Basilarchia archippus*)

Victoria 6:34R-M4

Violin
7:7R-M4

Vicuña 7:1R-MN

Victoria Regia (*V. regia*) 7:12R-WN

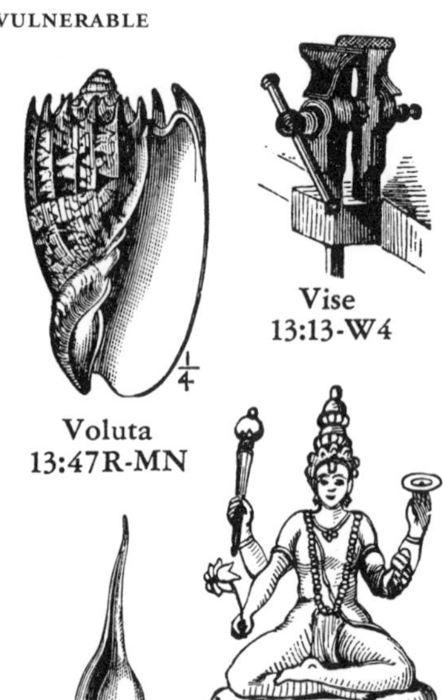

Vise
13:13-W4

Voluta
13:47R-MN

Visite
16:26R-W4

Vishnu 18:3R-W4

Volva volva
18:4-W

V

Voltaic Pile
18:20-MN

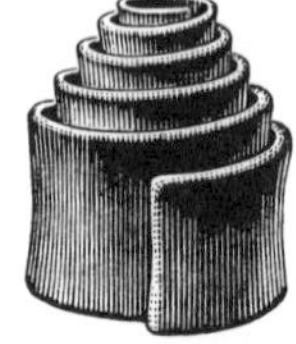

Volute Spring
18:18R-WN

W

Walking Stick
88.1 R-WN

Washer
88.9R-W4

Walking Fern
89.7R-MN

Walrus (*Trichecus rosmarus*) 90.3 R-MN

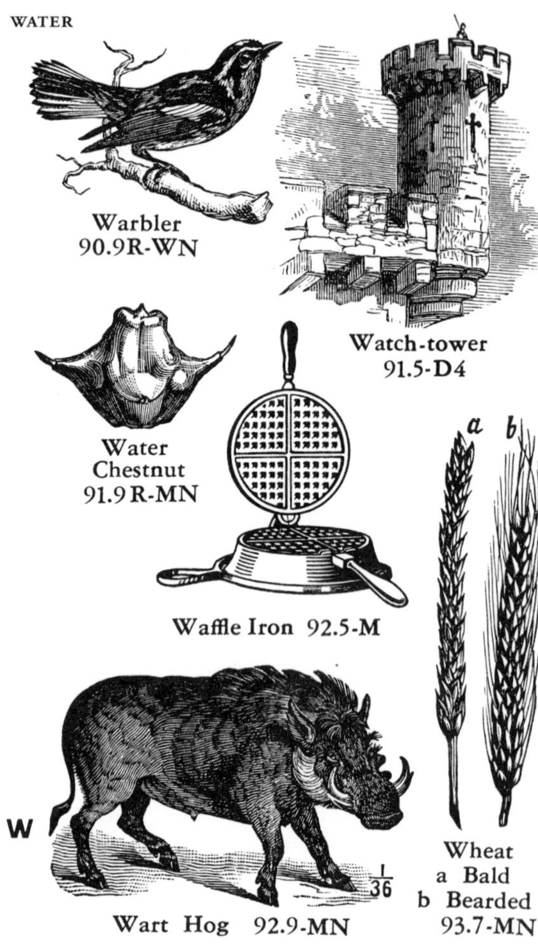

Warbler
90.9R-WN

Watch-tower
91.5-D4

Water
Chestnut
91.9 R-MN

Waffle Iron 92.5-M

Wheat
a Bald
b Bearded
93.7-MN

Wart Hog 92.9-MN

Water Spaniel
94.5R-WN

Wedge Shell
95.3-WN

Wax Palm 95.9R-W4

Wapiti 96.9R-MN

Whale 97.7-WN

W

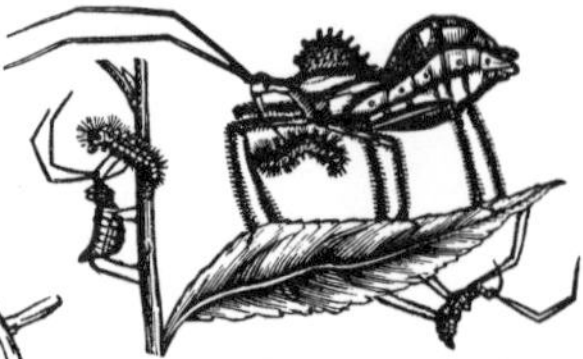

Wheel Bug 99.5-WN

Wheel 98.5R-W4

Wicker Basket
100.1-M

Wigwam 100.7-WN

W

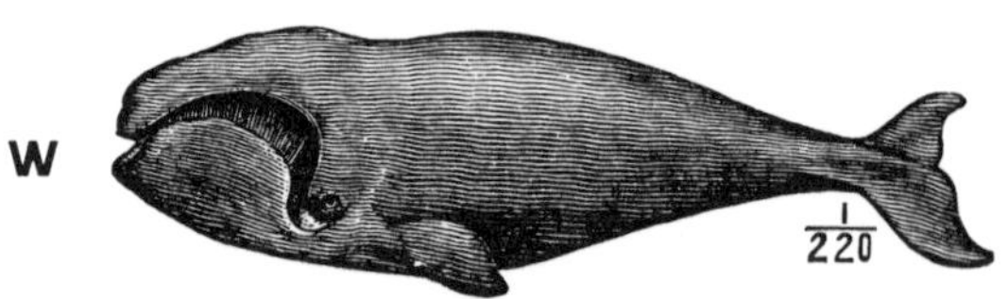

Whale (*Balæna cisarctica*) 101.7-MN

White Bear 102.5R-W
(*Ursus maritimus*)

Whistle
103.3R-MN

Windmill 104.1-W4

Windlass 105.7-WN

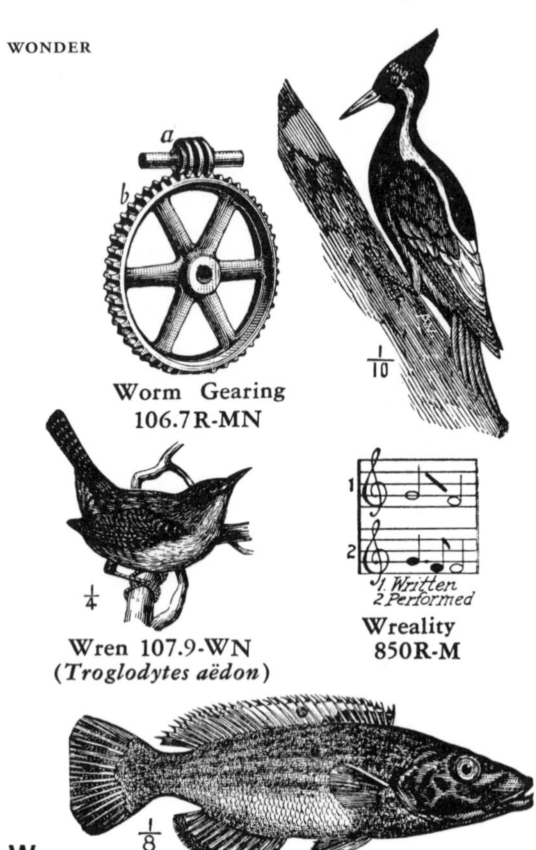

Worm Gearing
106.7R-MN

Wren 107.9-WN
(*Troglodytes aëdon*)

Wreality
850R-M

W

Wrasse (***Labrus trimaculatus***) 88.5-MN

Xebec 17-WN

Xiphioid (*Mesoplodon sowerbiensis*)
289-WN

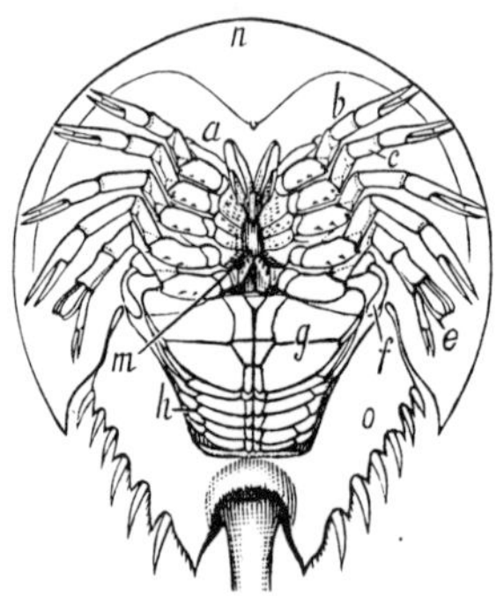

Xiphura 4913R-MN

Xylophone 83521R-MN

X

Yama 4042R-W4

Yapock 2780-WN

Yacare (*Jacare sclerops*) 228R-MN

Yellowthroat 4126R-MN
(*Geothlypis trichas*)

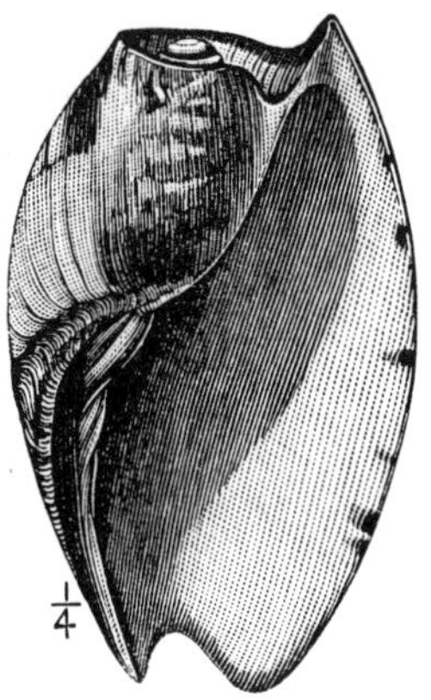

Yet 4241R-MN
(*Yetus cymbium*)

Yawl 6128R-ML

Y

Yew 4044-RW4
(*Taxus baccata*)

Yuen 4246R-MN
(*Hylobates pileatus*)

Z

Zebra (*Asinus zebra*) 61801-MN

Zamia
60637-WN

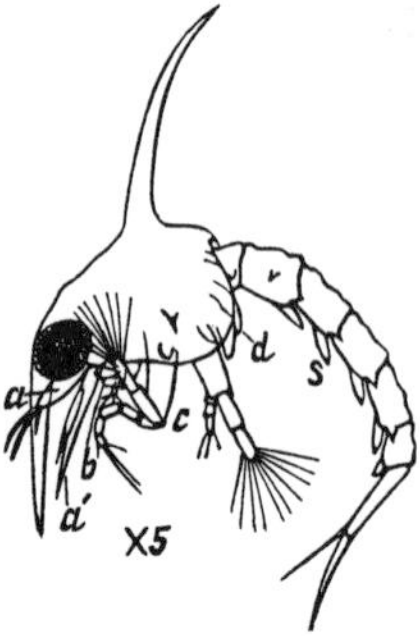

Zoëa
11786-WN
a Antennæ; b Jaws;
c Maxillipeds

Zebra Wolf 22046-M

Zeuglodon 44074-MN

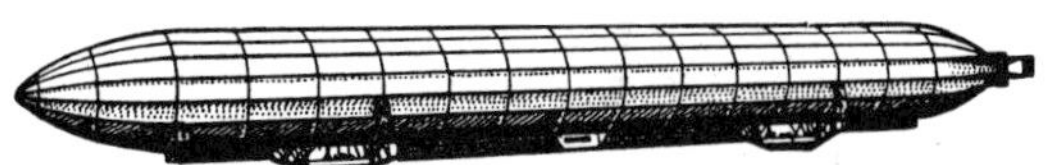

Zepplin 21704-M

Ziggurat 02139-ML

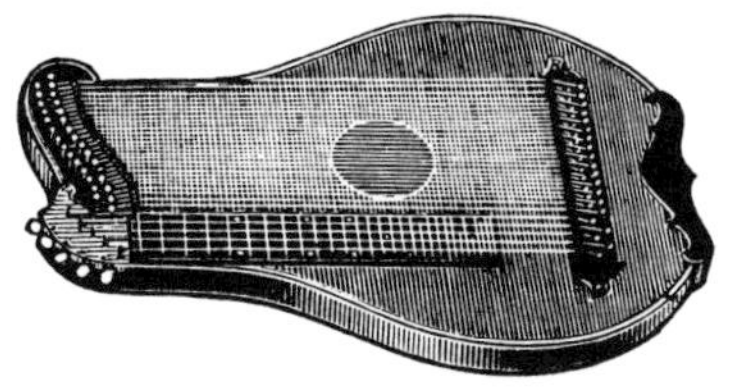

Zither 02154-MN

Zibeth 02453-WN

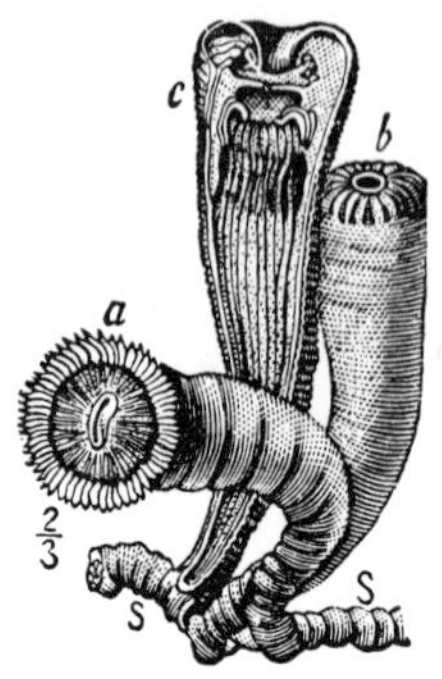

Zoanthus
(*Z. solanderi*)
02472-MN

Zodiac 21704-WN

COCCYX

Pictorial Webster's published for the first time the numbers stamped on the side of each of the wonderful dictionary engravings. These numbers were used to index and organize the engravings in a system of wooden cabinets at the G & C Merriam Co. The Pocket *Pictorial Webster's* assigns new numbers to the engravings to provide a new way to form associations with the images.

Numbers have meaning in every person's life. Phone numbers, license plate numbers, even my first credit card number have held dear places in my heart. My first Oberlin College Mail Room box number was 397 and I can still smell the sycamore leaves that fell on the ramp to the mail room when I see that number in print.

The images in each letter chapter of the *Pocket Pictorial* are organized by sequence, are part of a single long number, or are a collection of numbers belonging together for a reason that one might recognize. I have provided hints in the headings to help the reader guess what the numbers may reference. In a couple of instances I have used a combination of letters and numbers that are part of a code or convention that may be discovered. One of these codes provides additional hints.

See if you can unlock the 26 number sets. To find out more about the numbers in the book (and possibly win a prize), visit www.quercuspress.com.

ACKNOWLEDGMENTS

Thanks be to my wife, Carol, who made this book possible. This book is for her and for my children, Ember, Orion, and Arno. May the hours sacrificed now afford more time for us together. I love you.

Thanks to the great folks at Chronicle. Those I have met are Bridget Watson Payne, Eloise Leigh (my partner in crime), and Michael Carrabetta. I appreciate your hard work and the artistic freedom I received with the content of this book. Special thanks to Bill Hanscom for creating the *Pictorial Webster's* Garamond that made renumbering this book possible. Thanks to all of those who have given me encouragement these past couple of years of my life fraught with upheaval. My parents and sister, my friends, and strangers such as "Hank Dee" and the man I met at the Codex Symposium who told me he picks up *Pictorial Webster's* every day to find a little inspiration. Special thanks also to my "John" friends: Jon Ustun, Jon Calame, John Chamberlain, John Mason, and John Fisher for being there.

I am indebted to John Andrew and William Fowler Hopson and the editors of the G. & C. Merriam Company who were responsible for the creation of the images in this book. This has really been a century-long collaboration. Thanks also to my younger self who started *Pictorial Webster's* with none of the concerns that might have mired my more mature self. Here is hoping we can all maintain a youthful mindset . . . therein lies real hope.

Lophophore; 182R-W4 Arch Amphora Macaw Razor
Herringbone Masonry 2278-WN 302R-M4 Croton Bug C Egg Treble bone; Lacewing
Geranium Headearing Cringles Melanian Lungs 3146R-W4 Horse 2297R-MN
Dumb-Bell Scissors 234R-W4 (Pithecia Tam-tam Yacht
Toothshell Mechanics 3542R-MN end;
Ocelli; Flat; Eagle Stoup Mustella Wood screw (Eupagurus
Manicure; Sappho Sea Horse Banjo 162R-ML American Blockfish
Ambulacral Littorina Pocket; Wheel Seed 3299R-MN Lophiomys Maxilla (Paradisea 3105R-W4
Nail; 4 Button- Openings; Shaddock 3169R-W4 fibula; Triceratops
canadensis flabellum Palmatisected Hummingbird a Thread and (Radius
(Lophophorus Endosperm Prickly Pear (Megaptera Spire Thread Plant Lifeboat
Truncate Rhinoceros (Rhinolophus Lattice bellied) extruded; Forest Scape
Archaeopteryx Bird Jagged—though telarius) (Pelecanus Crooked (ML
Concretions 1024 Sea Grapes 2643R-MN Flower A Valve
(Strombus pugilis) 233R-W4 Cotter, fastening 2519-MN coiled Sea Crawfish
Altar 151R-MN Loop Tube Lant Jack (Pallifera dorsalis)
Valve 1757R-WN Serpula Carina 3431R-MN Pera- Head Crustacea 1193R-MN
Stork Single with Crook Lomentum Epicycloid
190R-W4 Plow 3314R-M Bee Bittle Swift 3246R-M4 House Lighthouse (Nelumbium Orifice
2915R-W4 Cylinder Lantern Bearded Dancer (Voluta musica) King Hypocycloid
Boiler; Q& Z Plectrum Compsognathus Tectibranchiata Heart Hippopotamus Cell
River Frostfish Tailor Bird Skipjack Diamond 3930R-M Spur Longirostres Sun wheel
Joint (Metridium dianthus) Cockroach Valvata
(Bornensis) Pegasus Jack Tarsometatarsus Sole Ichneumon
3332R-MN Fish (Vireo olivaceus) Courant Skull Ventral Medusa Trout
(Sphyrna tudes) Ray Flower Kangaroo Umbo Lantern Egg Vega Spectroscope 3674R-WN
A Focus of Potatoes (Tarsius spectrum) Irons dead. Bud Opened Setter (English) 3526R-MN
Type 1R-W4 (Carcharhinus obscurus) (Calluna vulgaris) Vibracula Limpets Veligera 2692-W
Swords Honey Roof Beams 3077R-WN Cocoa 534R-W4 Single Frogfish 1493R-MN
7106R-M Solar Microscope 2266-WN auricle Rocket Right Starting Baltimore Oriole 433R-MN
2743R-MN Manus of Tapir Manus of Horse (Oaks) Conch Safety
1732R-WN Venus's Basket Tree Climbing Fish White 1383R-W4
Arrow 200R-W4 Sea Involucre Electric Fish Queen Rose Tulip 3918R-MN
Yaks 169R-MN Involute lateralis) Involucre (Torpedo Quercus (M.
Bayonet Rose Telescope Centers Lugger 2458-WN Perch Case 3523-M
Vampire) Weever Grates Lintel Overflow Lion 6401R-ME Crab 4359R-MN
(Longimanus Mountain Magnet Poplar (Felis Artillary from a Cell Jack Boot
Fleur-de-lis Lumbar Loup-de-loup aeruginosa) Tulip prolifera) Cerastes Order Jack Boot
Loup-de-loup Banjo Pagoda Weight, 3641R-WN Stocks Pumps Limpet
Tailor 1775R-MN Goby Victorine (Mactra Lieutenant Lieutenant Scissors Skate
Flower Horse Lantern officinale) Umbelliferae Bivalve
(americanus) Lyre Bird Triton Scattered Pumps; Atoll
Queen, Lantern Fly (Triton perspicillata) Insect Throat 1381R
(Terminalia indica) Penumbra Reverse Arms Bastion
Isotherms A Sexual individual Cupola Furnace Tube Fish Indian Comptera 3038R-M
R-MN Victorine 108-MN (Pandanus) Plane can Violets Tom Flower Fish
Loris Weights 406R-MN Skate Vulture Knight Sulky Sucker Flower Keel;
Layers (Sarcophilus ursinus) Lantern Square Stoup sciurus) Right Right (Arbutum
1356-W Land Crab Mountain Manatee Gastric (Ovatus) ausi) Aerodrome Katydid
Pterocerus 1768-W Hyena Rhinolophid Fess Setiform Karyokinesis (Anodonta naevia) (Jasmine Cotyledons;
Abacus Claws; Hyena Indris